The Nasdaq DJT Playbook: Understanding and Profiting from the Transportation Sector

Table of Contents

Introduction

- Overview of the Nasdaq DJT and Its Significance
- History and Evolution of the Dow Jones Transportation Average (DJT)
- The Importance of the Transportation Sector in the Global Economy

Chapter 1: Understanding the Nasdaq DJT

- What is the Nasdaq DJT and How Does It Work?
- Key Components of the DJT Index
- How the DJT Index is Calculated
- Differences Between the Nasdaq DJT and Other Market Indices

Chapter 2: Analyzing the Transportation Sector

- Overview of the Transportation Sector: Airlines, Railroads, Shipping, and Logistics
- Economic Impact of the Transportation Industry
- Factors Influencing the Sector's Performance (e.g., Oil Prices, Regulations, Technological Innovations)

Chapter 3: History and Performance of the Nasdaq DJT

- Historical Analysis of the Nasdaq DJT's Performance
- Booms and Busts: Lessons from the Past
- How the DJT Compares to Other Market Indices

Chapter 4: Investment Strategies for the Nasdaq DJT

- Long-Term Investment Approaches in the Nasdaq DJT
- Short-Term Trading Techniques and Strategies
- Using ETFs and Mutual Funds Related to the DJT
- Portfolio Diversification with the Inclusion of the Nasdaq DJT

Chapter 5: Technical and Fundamental Analysis of the Nasdaq DJT

- How to Conduct Technical Analysis on the DJT
- Key Technical Indicators Used in Nasdaq DJT Trading
- Fundamental Analysis: Evaluating the DJT's Component Companies
- Reading Financial Statements and Assessing Future Prospects

Chapter 6: Macroeconomic Factors and the Nasdaq DJT

- How Macroeconomic Changes Influence the DJT
- The Impact of Monetary and Fiscal Policies
- Globalization and the Future of the Transportation Sector

Chapter 7: Case Studies of Success and Failure

- Analyzing Successful Companies within the DJT
- Lessons from Failures and Crises in the Transportation Sector
- Identifying Opportunities and Risks

Chapter 8: The Future of the Nasdaq DJT

- Emerging Trends in the Transportation Sector (e.g., Autonomous Vehicles, Sustainability)
- How These Trends Could Impact the Nasdaq DJT
- Forecasts and Future Scenarios for the Index

Conclusion

- Final Reflections and Investment Tips
- The Importance of a Long-Term Perspective
- How to Stay Informed and Keep Up with Nasdaq DJT Trends

Introduction

The Nasdaq DJT, officially known as the Dow Jones Transportation Average (DJT), is not just one of the oldest stock indices in the world—it's a vital indicator that reflects the heartbeat of the global economy. As a barometer for the performance of the transportation sector, the DJT encapsulates the dynamic movements of airlines, railroads, shipping companies, and logistics firms. These industries are the backbone of the world's economic infrastructure, ensuring the continuous flow of goods and people across continents.

Imagine the world without an efficient transportation sector: products would languish in warehouses, supply chains would grind to a halt, and economies would struggle to function. The DJT, therefore, is more than just an index; it's a critical gauge of economic health and an essential tool for investors seeking to understand broader market trends.

In this book, you will embark on a journey through the intricacies of the Nasdaq DJT. We will demystify how this index functions, explore its historical performance, and dive into the strategies that can help you profit from investing in this dynamic sector. Whether you're a seasoned investor looking to diversify your portfolio or a newcomer eager to understand a vital segment of the market, this book will equip you with the tools and knowledge you need to navigate the complexities of the DJT.

The Nasdaq DJT: A Historical Perspective

The origins of the Dow Jones Transportation Average date back to 1884 when Charles Dow, co-founder of Dow Jones & Company and The Wall Street Journal, introduced this index. Initially composed of nine railroad companies and two non-railroad entities, the DJT was designed to track the performance of the burgeoning transportation industry, which was at the time dominated by railroads.

Fast forward to today, and the Nasdaq DJT has evolved to reflect the modern dynamics of the transportation sector. It now tracks the performance of 20 leading transportation companies, encompassing a broad array of industries, from aviation to logistics. This evolution mirrors the changing landscape of global transportation—what once was a railroad-centric index now provides a snapshot of a diversified and crucial economic sector.

Example: Consider the historical significance of the railroad companies in the late 19th century. At that time, the expansion of the railroad network across the United States was a major driver of economic growth, much like how the rise of logistics giants such as FedEx and UPS has become vital in today's globalized economy. The DJT has adapted to these changes, offering investors a window into the industries that move the world.

Why the Transportation Sector Matters

The transportation sector is the linchpin of global commerce. It connects manufacturers with consumers, facilitates international trade, and supports the infrastructure that drives economic growth. The performance of transportation companies often provides early signals about broader economic trends. For instance, an increase in freight shipments typically indicates rising consumer demand, while a decline might signal an impending economic slowdown.

Investing in the Nasdaq DJT is not just about tracking individual companies; it's about understanding the macroeconomic forces that drive the sector. Factors such as oil prices, regulatory changes, technological advancements, and global trade policies play significant roles in shaping the fortunes of transportation companies. By understanding these factors, investors can make more informed decisions and capitalize on the opportunities presented by this sector.

Example: The impact of fluctuating oil prices on the transportation sector cannot be overstated. For example, a sharp increase in oil prices can lead to higher operational costs for airlines and shipping companies, squeezing profit margins and potentially leading to reduced stock prices for these companies within the DJT. Conversely, technological advancements, such as the development of more fuel-efficient aircraft, can mitigate these effects and boost investor confidence in the sector.

What You Will Learn

This book is designed to be a comprehensive guide to the Nasdaq DJT. It covers everything from the basics of how the index is calculated to advanced investment strategies tailored to the transportation sector. Here's what you can expect:

Understanding the Index: Learn what the Nasdaq DJT is, how it is structured, and why it is a crucial part of the financial landscape. Discover how the index's components are selected and the weighting method used to ensure it accurately reflects the sector's performance.

Analyzing the Sector: Dive into the different components of the transportation sector, including airlines, railroads, and shipping companies, and understand the economic forces that drive them. We'll explore case studies of how companies like Delta Air Lines and Union Pacific have navigated economic cycles, adapting to challenges and seizing opportunities.

Investment Strategies: Explore long-term and short-term strategies for investing in the Nasdaq DJT, including the use of ETFs and mutual funds, and how to diversify your portfolio effectively. Whether you're a buy-and-hold investor or a day trader, we'll provide actionable insights to help you maximize your returns.

Technical and Fundamental Analysis: Gain insights into both technical and fundamental analysis techniques that can help you make smarter investment decisions. We'll walk you through key technical indicators, such as moving averages and relative strength index (RSI), and how to apply them to DJT components like FedEx or CSX Corporation.

Macroeconomic Influences: Understand how broader economic trends, such as changes in monetary policy or shifts in global trade, impact the Nasdaq DJT. Learn how events like the U.S.-China trade war or interest rate changes by the Federal Reserve can create ripples across the transportation sector.

Case Studies and Future Trends: Learn from real-world examples of success and failure within the sector and explore emerging trends that could shape the future of the index. We'll analyze the rise of e-commerce and its impact on logistics companies, and how autonomous vehicles might revolutionize the transportation landscape.

A Journey Worth Taking

Investing in the Nasdaq DJT offers a unique opportunity to participate in a sector that is essential to the functioning of the global economy. However, like any investment, it requires knowledge, strategy, and a willingness to adapt to changing conditions. This book aims to equip you with the understanding and tools you need to navigate the complexities of the Nasdaq DJT and make informed investment decisions.

As you progress through this book, you'll not only gain a deeper appreciation for the transportation sector but also discover how it can be a valuable addition to your investment portfolio. The journey begins here—let's explore the Nasdaq DJT together and unlock its potential for growth and profitability.

Example: Imagine the potential of being ahead of the curve in recognizing the significance of autonomous trucking. As this technology develops, companies leading this innovation could see substantial growth. Understanding these trends and their impact on the DJT could position you to make strategic investments that capitalize on the next wave of advancements in transportation.

Chapter 1: Understanding the Nasdaq DJT

The Nasdaq DJT, or Dow Jones Transportation Average, is more than just an index; it is a crucial indicator of the global transportation sector's health and a reflection of broader economic trends. To fully appreciate the significance of the DJT, it is essential to understand its structure, the key components it tracks, and the methodology behind its calculation. This chapter will provide an in-depth exploration of what the Nasdaq DJT is, how it operates, and why it remains an indispensable tool for investors seeking insights into the transportation industry.

What is the Nasdaq DJT and How Does It Work?

The Nasdaq DJT, established in 1884, holds the distinction of being one of the oldest stock indices in the world. Originally created by Charles Dow, one of the founders of Dow Jones & Company, the DJT was designed to track the performance of the transportation sector—a vital component of the global economy. Today, it specifically monitors the performance of 20 major transportation companies across various industries, including airlines, railroads, trucking, and shipping.

The DJT's role as a barometer of the transportation industry cannot be overstated. The transportation sector is intrinsically linked to the movement of goods and people, making it a critical indicator of economic activity. When transportation companies thrive, it often signals a robust economy with high consumer demand and strong industrial output. Conversely, a decline in transportation activity can be an early warning of economic slowdown, as it suggests reduced demand for goods and services.

Example: The 2008 financial crisis serves as a poignant example of the DJT's role in reflecting broader economic conditions. As the global economy contracted, demand for goods and services plummeted, leading to a significant decline in transportation activities. The DJT mirrored this downturn, with a sharp drop in its value as transportation companies across the sector faced reduced revenues and profitability. This decline was not just a reflection of the transportation sector's struggles, but also a broader indication of the economic challenges facing industries worldwide. Conversely, during periods of economic recovery, such as the post-crisis expansion in the early 2010s, the DJT often shows strong performance, driven by increased demand for transportation services as economic activity rebounds.

Key Components of the DJT Index

The Nasdaq DJT is composed of 20 carefully selected transportation companies that represent the diverse industries within the sector. These companies are chosen to provide a comprehensive view of the transportation industry, capturing the various facets of how goods and people move across the globe. The components of the DJT include some of the largest and most influential players in transportation, each playing a vital role in their respective industries.

Airlines: Airlines are a significant component of the DJT, with major players like Delta Air Lines and Southwest Airlines included in the index. Airlines are highly sensitive to economic changes, fuel prices, and consumer demand for travel. During periods of economic growth, airlines typically experience increased passenger numbers and cargo shipments, leading to higher revenues. However, they are also vulnerable to downturns, as seen during the COVID-19 pandemic, when travel restrictions led to unprecedented declines in airline revenues.

Railroads: Railroads are often considered the backbone of the transportation sector, essential for the movement of bulk goods across vast distances. Companies such as Union Pacific and Norfolk Southern dominate the railroad segment of the DJT. Railroads play a crucial role in industries like agriculture, mining, and manufacturing, where large quantities of raw materials and finished goods need to be transported efficiently. The health of the railroad industry is often a bellwether for industrial activity, making it a key component of the DJT.

Trucking: The trucking industry is represented in the DJT by companies like J.B. Hunt Transport Services, which play a crucial role in the last-mile delivery of goods. Trucking connects manufacturers with retailers and consumers, ensuring that goods reach their final destination. The trucking industry is highly responsive to changes in consumer demand, as it is directly involved in the distribution of goods across the country. In recent years, the rise of e-commerce has significantly increased the demand for trucking services, highlighting the industry's importance in the modern economy.

Shipping and Logistics: The DJT also includes giants like FedEx and United Parcel Service (UPS), underscoring the importance of global logistics and shipping in modern commerce. These companies are integral to the global supply chain, facilitating the movement of goods across international borders. The performance of shipping and logistics companies is closely tied to global trade volumes, making them a critical component of the DJT. The surge in e-commerce during the COVID-19 pandemic highlighted the pivotal role of logistics companies, as they stepped up to meet the increased demand for home deliveries.

Example: The divergent performance of different DJT components during the COVID-19 pandemic offers a clear illustration of the index's ability to provide a nuanced view of the transportation sector. While airlines suffered significant losses due to travel restrictions, logistics companies like UPS and FedEx experienced increased demand as consumers shifted to online shopping. This divergence within the DJT components highlights the importance of understanding the individual industries within the index, as well as the broader economic forces at play.

How the DJT Index is Calculated

Understanding how the DJT is calculated is crucial for interpreting its movements and making informed investment decisions. Unlike many other indices that are weighted by market capitalization, the DJT is a price-weighted index. This means that companies with higher stock prices have a greater influence on the index's movements, regardless of their overall market value.

Price-Weighted Index: In a price-weighted index like the DJT, the stock prices of the component companies are added together and then divided by a divisor. The divisor is adjusted periodically to account for stock splits, dividends, and other corporate actions that might affect the stock prices. The price-weighted approach gives more influence to companies with higher stock prices, which can lead to significant swings in the index if those companies experience large price movements.

Example: Consider a scenario where Delta Air Lines has a stock price of $40, and Union Pacific's stock is priced at $200. Even if Delta's market capitalization is larger, Union Pacific will have a greater impact on the DJT's value due to its higher stock price. This price-weighted approach means that changes in the stock prices of more expensive stocks can significantly sway the DJT, making it important for investors to understand which companies hold more sway within the index.

Divisor Adjustments: The DJT's divisor is not a fixed number. It is adjusted whenever there are stock splits, dividends, or other corporate actions to ensure that such events do not artificially alter the value of the index. For example, if a company within the DJT undergoes a 2-for-1 stock split, the stock price would halve, but the company's market value would remain the same. To prevent this change from impacting the overall index value, the divisor would be adjusted accordingly. This adjustment process makes the DJT a more accurate reflection of the transportation sector's performance over time, allowing it to provide a consistent measure of industry health.

Differences Between the Nasdaq DJT and Other Market Indices

While the DJT is a critical index for the transportation sector, it is essential to understand how it differs from other major market indices, such as the Dow Jones Industrial Average (DJIA) and the S&P 500. These differences highlight the unique role that the DJT plays in providing insights into the transportation industry and the broader economy.

Sector-Specific Focus: The DJT's primary focus on transportation sets it apart from broader indices like the DJIA or the S&P 500, which encompass a wide range of industries. This sector-specific focus allows investors to gain detailed insights into transportation trends, which can be used to predict broader economic movements. For example, an increase in freight shipments might signal rising consumer demand, while a decline in airline passenger numbers could indicate economic uncertainty. The DJT's focus on transportation makes it a valuable tool for investors seeking to understand the economic forces that drive this vital sector.

Historical Significance: The DJT, as one of the oldest indices, has a rich history that offers long-term data on the transportation sector. This historical perspective is invaluable for identifying trends and understanding the cyclical nature of the industry. By studying the DJT's historical performance, investors can gain insights into how the transportation sector responds to different economic conditions, from periods of rapid growth to times of recession.

Example: During periods of economic uncertainty, such as the dot-com bubble burst in the early 2000s, the DJT often provided early signals of economic distress as transportation companies began to experience declines before other sectors. This early warning capability is one of the reasons why the DJT is closely watched by economists and investors alike. Conversely, during economic recoveries, the DJT has often been one of the first indices to show signs of improvement, as the demand for transportation services picks up. This was evident in the aftermath of the 2008 financial crisis, when the DJT began to recover ahead of other indices, signaling a broader economic rebound.

Broader Economic Insights: While the DJT focuses on transportation, its performance is closely tied to broader economic conditions. For instance, the DJT's response to changes in oil prices, government regulations, and global trade policies can provide valuable insights into the overall health of the economy. Investors who closely monitor the DJT can gain a deeper understanding of how these macroeconomic factors impact the transportation sector and, by extension, the broader market.

Example: The rise of global trade tensions, such as those between the United States and China, has had a significant impact on the DJT. As tariffs and trade barriers were introduced, companies involved in international shipping and logistics faced increased costs and uncertainty, which was reflected in their stock prices and, consequently, in the DJT's performance. By understanding these broader economic influences, investors can anticipate potential risks and opportunities within the transportation sector.

Chapter 2: Analyzing the Transportation Sector

The transportation sector is a cornerstone of the global economy, encompassing a wide array of industries that are vital for the movement of goods, people, and services across the world. This sector includes everything from passenger airlines and freight railroads to trucking companies and global shipping giants. Each segment of the transportation industry plays a distinct role in supporting economic activity, and their performance is closely tied to broader market trends. In this chapter, we will explore the various components of the transportation sector, the economic forces that drive them, and how these industries interact with the global economy. We'll use detailed examples to illustrate how changes within this sector can signal shifts in economic conditions and influence investment strategies.

Overview of the Transportation Sector

The transportation sector is diverse and multifaceted, with industries that range from the large-scale movement of goods across oceans to the last-mile delivery of packages to consumers' doorsteps. Each of these industries has its own dynamics, influenced by factors such as fuel costs, regulatory changes, technological advancements, and consumer demand. Understanding these dynamics is crucial for investors who want to anticipate changes in the sector and make informed investment decisions.

Airlines

The airline industry is a major component of the transportation sector, playing a critical role in connecting people and businesses across the globe. Airlines are responsible for the rapid movement of passengers and cargo over long distances, making them essential to both business and leisure travel. However, the airline industry is particularly sensitive to several external factors, including changes in fuel prices, economic conditions, and geopolitical events.

Example: The impact of fuel prices on the airline industry is profound. In 2014, a dramatic drop in oil prices led to a significant reduction in fuel costs for airlines, which typically account for a substantial portion of their operating expenses. This reduction in costs resulted in higher profit margins for airlines, leading to a surge in their stock prices. For instance, Delta Air Lines and American Airlines saw substantial increases in their share prices during this period as investors anticipated improved profitability. Conversely, the spike in oil prices in 2008, before the financial crisis, had the opposite effect. Airlines faced soaring fuel costs, which squeezed profit margins and forced them to raise ticket prices or cut routes. This, in turn, led to a decline in demand for air travel, illustrating how closely airline performance is tied to fluctuations in fuel prices.

Example: The airline industry is also highly sensitive to geopolitical events. For instance, the outbreak of the Gulf War in 1990 caused a sharp increase in oil prices, which, combined with fears of terrorism and the general uncertainty of war, led to a significant drop in air travel. Airlines faced reduced demand, leading to widespread layoffs and financial difficulties. Similarly, the 9/11 attacks in 2001 had a profound and long-lasting impact on the airline industry. In the immediate aftermath, air travel plummeted due to safety concerns and tighter security measures, causing significant financial losses for airlines worldwide.

Railroads

The railroad industry is a backbone of freight transportation, particularly in regions with extensive rail networks like North America. Railroads are essential for transporting bulk goods such as coal, agricultural products, and industrial materials over long distances. This industry is highly capital-intensive, requiring significant investments in infrastructure and equipment. Railroads also benefit from economies of scale, making them one of the most efficient modes of land transportation for heavy and bulk goods.

Example: Union Pacific, one of the largest railroad companies in the United States, plays a vital role in transporting goods from agricultural regions in the Midwest to ports on the West Coast. A surge in demand for agricultural exports to Asia, driven by favorable trade agreements, can lead to increased revenues for Union Pacific as more goods are shipped via rail to ports for international export. This not only boosts the company's earnings but also highlights the critical role railroads play in supporting international trade. Conversely, a decline in coal consumption due to environmental regulations has negatively impacted railroads that rely heavily on coal shipments. As seen in recent years, the transition towards cleaner energy sources has led to a reduction in coal transport, forcing railroads to adapt by diversifying their cargo.

Example: Railroads are also affected by changes in the industrial economy. During periods of economic expansion, there is typically an increase in the production of goods such as automobiles, steel, and construction materials—all of which are transported by rail. For example, during the economic boom of the early 2000s, railroads experienced strong demand as manufacturing activity increased.

However, during economic downturns, such as the Great Recession of 2008-2009, the demand for these goods declined, leading to a corresponding decrease in rail traffic. This cyclical nature of the railroad industry underscores the importance of monitoring industrial production trends when analyzing railroad stocks.

Trucking

The trucking industry is crucial for the final leg of supply chains, delivering goods from warehouses to retail stores and directly to consumers. Trucking companies handle a significant portion of domestic freight, making them indispensable for the movement of goods across short and medium distances. The rise of e-commerce has significantly increased the demand for trucking services, particularly for last-mile delivery, where goods are transported from distribution centers to their final destinations. However, the trucking industry also faces challenges, including driver shortages, regulatory changes, and fluctuations in fuel prices.

Example: The impact of e-commerce on the trucking industry is profound. Companies like Amazon have transformed consumer expectations, leading to an increase in demand for fast and reliable delivery services. This shift has benefited trucking companies like J.B. Hunt Transport Services, which have expanded their operations to meet the growing need for last-mile delivery. For instance, J.B. Hunt has invested in advanced logistics systems and expanded its fleet to handle the increased volume of packages generated by online shopping. However, the industry also faces challenges such as driver shortages, which can lead to higher labor costs and impact profitability. The shortage of qualified truck drivers has been a persistent issue in the industry, exacerbated by the aging workforce and the high turnover rate. This shortage has driven up wages, increased recruitment costs, and, in some cases, led to delays in delivery times.

Example: Regulatory changes also have a significant impact on the trucking industry. For instance, the implementation of the Electronic Logging Device (ELD) mandate by the U.S. Federal Motor Carrier Safety Administration (FMCSA) in 2017 required trucking companies to install electronic devices that monitor the driving hours of truck drivers. This regulation aimed to improve road safety by ensuring compliance with hours-of-service rules. However, the mandate also led to increased costs for trucking companies, both in terms of purchasing and installing the devices and in the potential loss of productivity as drivers were forced to take longer rest periods. Smaller trucking companies, in particular, struggled with the financial burden of compliance, leading some to exit the industry altogether.

Shipping and Logistics

Shipping and logistics companies are the arteries of global trade, ensuring the smooth flow of goods across international borders. These companies manage complex supply chains, coordinating the movement of products from manufacturers to end consumers. The performance of shipping and logistics companies is closely tied to global trade volumes, making them sensitive to changes in trade policies, tariffs, and economic conditions.

Example: The impact of global trade tensions on shipping and logistics companies can be significant. For instance, during the U.S.-China trade war, companies like FedEx and UPS faced increased uncertainty as tariffs and trade barriers disrupted supply chains. These disruptions often led to shifts in trade routes, delays, and increased costs, which were reflected in the financial performance of these companies and, by extension, in the DJT's overall performance. For example, FedEx reported lower-than-expected earnings in 2019, attributing the decline to weaker global trade volumes and the impact of tariffs on its international business. The uncertainty surrounding trade negotiations also led some companies to reroute shipments or stockpile inventory, further complicating logistics operations.

Example: The shipping industry is also highly susceptible to changes in global economic conditions. During periods of economic expansion, the demand for shipping services increases as global trade volumes rise. For instance, the economic boom in China during the early 2000s led to a surge in demand for shipping services, as the country became a major exporter of manufactured goods. Shipping companies like Maersk and Mediterranean Shipping Company (MSC) expanded their fleets and increased capacity to meet the growing demand. However, during economic downturns, such as the global recession of 2008-2009, shipping volumes declined sharply, leading to overcapacity and falling freight rates. The Baltic Dry Index, a key indicator of global shipping costs, plummeted during this period, reflecting the steep decline in demand for bulk shipping.

Economic Forces Driving the Transportation Sector

The transportation sector is influenced by a variety of economic forces that can affect its performance in both the short and long term. These forces include fuel prices, regulatory changes, technological advancements, and consumer demand. Understanding these forces is crucial for investors who want to anticipate changes in the sector and make informed investment decisions.

Fuel Prices

One of the most significant factors affecting the transportation sector is the price of fuel. Fuel costs directly impact the profitability of airlines, trucking companies, and shipping firms, making them highly sensitive to fluctuations in oil prices. When fuel prices rise, transportation companies often face higher operational costs, which can squeeze profit margins and lead to higher prices for consumers. Conversely, when fuel prices fall, transportation companies can benefit from reduced costs, leading to improved profitability.

Example: During the oil price spike in 2008, transportation companies across the board faced increased costs. Airlines, in particular, were hard hit, as fuel typically accounts for a large portion of their operating expenses. Many airlines implemented fuel surcharges, reduced capacity, or even grounded less fuel-efficient aircraft in response to the rising costs. The trucking industry also felt the impact, with smaller operators struggling to stay afloat due to the sudden increase in fuel expenses. Some trucking companies passed on the higher costs to customers through fuel surcharges, while others were forced to cut back on operations. Conversely, the dramatic drop in oil prices in 2014 provided a temporary boost to the sector, with reduced fuel costs leading to higher profitability and stock prices for many transportation companies.

Example: The shipping industry is also heavily influenced by fuel prices. The introduction of low-sulfur fuel regulations under IMO 2020 further increased costs for shipping companies, as they were required to switch to more expensive, cleaner-burning fuels. This regulation aimed to reduce sulfur emissions from ships, which are a major source of air pollution. Some shipping companies invested in scrubbers, devices that remove sulfur from exhaust gases, to continue using cheaper high-sulfur fuel. Others passed on the higher fuel costs to customers through increased freight rates. The introduction of these regulations highlights how fuel prices and environmental regulations can interact to shape the financial performance of the transportation sector.

Regulatory Changes

Government regulations play a significant role in shaping the transportation sector. Regulations can impact everything from safety standards to environmental policies, and changes in these regulations can have wide-reaching effects on the industry. For example, stricter emissions standards may require transportation companies to invest in new, more efficient technologies, leading to increased costs but also potential long-term savings and environmental benefits.

Example: The implementation of stricter emissions regulations by the International Maritime Organization (IMO) in 2020, known as IMO 2020, required shipping companies to reduce the sulfur content in their fuel. This regulation led to significant changes in the industry, as companies had to either invest in new ships with cleaner engines or retrofit existing vessels with scrubbers to reduce emissions. The transition came with increased costs, but it also presented opportunities for companies that were early adopters of cleaner technologies to gain a competitive advantage. For instance, Maersk, one of the largest shipping companies in the world, invested heavily in new, more efficient vessels that complied with the IMO 2020 regulations. This early investment allowed Maersk to maintain its market leadership while meeting the new environmental standards.

Example: The transportation sector is also subject to safety regulations, which can impact operations and profitability. For instance, the Federal Aviation Administration (FAA) in the United States imposes strict safety standards on airlines, requiring regular maintenance, inspections, and certifications. Compliance with these regulations is costly but essential for ensuring passenger safety and maintaining public confidence in air travel. In some cases, regulatory changes can have a significant impact on the industry. For example, the grounding of the Boeing 737 Max aircraft in 2019, following two fatal crashes, led to significant disruptions for airlines that operated the aircraft. Airlines had to cancel flights, reconfigure schedules, and lease replacement aircraft, leading to increased costs and lost revenues.

Technological Advancements

Technology is rapidly transforming the transportation sector, with innovations ranging from autonomous vehicles to more fuel-efficient engines. These advancements have the potential to significantly impact the industry, reducing costs, increasing efficiency, and opening up new business opportunities. However, they also pose challenges, as companies must invest in new technologies and adapt to changing market dynamics.

Example: The development of autonomous trucks has the potential to revolutionize the trucking industry. Companies like Tesla and Waymo are at the forefront of this technology, which promises to reduce labor costs, increase safety, and improve fuel efficiency. Autonomous trucks can operate continuously without the need for rest breaks, increasing productivity and reducing delivery times. However, the widespread adoption of autonomous trucks also raises concerns about job losses in the trucking industry and the need for new regulatory frameworks to ensure safety on the roads. The impact of this technology on companies within the DJT will likely be significant, with those that can successfully integrate autonomous vehicles into their operations gaining a competitive edge.

Example: The aviation industry is also seeing significant technological advancements, particularly in the development of more fuel-efficient aircraft. Boeing and Airbus, the two largest aircraft manufacturers, have both introduced new models designed to reduce fuel consumption and lower operating costs. For example, the Boeing 787 Dreamliner and the Airbus A350 are built with lightweight composite materials and advanced aerodynamics, making them more fuel-efficient than previous generations of aircraft. Airlines that invest in these newer, more efficient models can benefit from lower fuel costs and increased profitability. However, the high cost of purchasing new aircraft can be a barrier for some airlines, leading them to explore other options, such as retrofitting existing fleets with more efficient engines or leasing newer models.

Consumer Demand

Consumer demand is a key driver of the transportation sector, influencing everything from airline passenger numbers to the volume of goods shipped by truck or rail. Changes in consumer behavior, driven by factors such as economic conditions, technological advancements, and shifting preferences, can have a direct impact on the performance of transportation companies.

Example: The rise of e-commerce has dramatically altered consumer expectations, leading to increased demand for fast and reliable delivery services. This shift has benefited logistics companies like UPS and FedEx, which have expanded their operations to meet the growing need for last-mile delivery. For instance, UPS has invested heavily in its logistics network, including the use of advanced tracking systems and automated sorting facilities, to ensure that packages are delivered quickly and efficiently. However, the same trend has also put pressure on traditional brick-and-mortar retailers, who must now compete with online giants by offering comparable delivery options. Retailers have had to adapt by offering same-day or next-day delivery services, often at a significant cost, to meet consumer expectations.

Example: The airline industry is also influenced by changes in consumer demand. During periods of economic growth, consumers are more likely to spend money on travel, leading to increased demand for air travel. For example, the global economic expansion in the early 2000s led to a boom in air travel, with airlines adding new routes and increasing capacity to meet the growing demand. However, during economic downturns, such as the Great Recession of 2008-2009, consumers cut back on discretionary spending, including travel, leading to a decline in airline revenues. The COVID-

19 pandemic had an even more dramatic impact, as travel restrictions and health concerns led to a collapse in demand for air travel. Airlines were forced to ground fleets, lay off employees, and seek government bailouts to survive the crisis.

Interdependence of Transportation Segments

One of the key characteristics of the transportation sector is the interdependence of its various segments. Airlines, railroads, trucking, and shipping are all interconnected, with the performance of one segment often influencing the others. Understanding this interdependence is crucial for investors, as it allows them to anticipate how changes in one part of the sector might ripple through the entire industry.

Example: The relationship between railroads and shipping is a prime example of this interdependence. Many goods transported by rail are ultimately destined for international markets, making ports and shipping companies critical links in the supply chain. For example, agricultural products grown in the Midwest United States are often transported by rail to ports on the West Coast, where they are then shipped to markets in Asia. When port congestion occurs, it can delay the movement of goods by rail, leading to increased costs and potential bottlenecks throughout the supply chain. Conversely, a surge in international trade can boost demand for rail services as more goods need to be transported from inland producers to coastal ports for export. Understanding these connections allows investors to see the bigger picture and make more informed decisions about where to allocate their resources.

Example: Another example of interdependence is the relationship between the trucking and e-commerce sectors. The rise of e-commerce has led to increased demand for last-mile delivery services, which has, in turn, driven growth in the trucking industry. Companies like Amazon have built extensive logistics networks that rely heavily on trucking to move goods from fulfillment centers to consumers. However, disruptions in the supply chain, such as those caused by the COVID-19 pandemic, can have a ripple effect throughout the entire transportation sector. For example, delays in the production of goods due to factory shutdowns can lead to reduced demand for trucking services, as there are fewer goods to transport. Similarly, disruptions in shipping can delay the arrival of goods at distribution centers, leading to delays in last-mile delivery and impacting consumer satisfaction.

Example: The aviation and tourism industries are also closely interconnected. Airlines rely heavily on tourism for a significant portion of their revenue, particularly during peak travel seasons. Conversely, the tourism industry depends on airlines to bring travelers to destinations around the world. When air travel declines, as it did during the COVID-19 pandemic, it not only impacts airlines but also has a cascading effect on hotels, restaurants, and other businesses that rely on tourism. The interdependence of these industries underscores the importance of a holistic approach to investing in the transportation sector, taking into account the broader economic and social factors that influence demand.

Chapter 3: Historical Performance of the Nasdaq DJT

The historical performance of the Nasdaq DJT (Dow Jones Transportation Average) offers invaluable insights into the transportation sector's evolution and its role as a barometer of economic health. By examining key trends, market cycles, and significant events that have shaped the DJT over the decades, investors can better understand how this index reacts to various economic forces. This chapter delves into the historical data of the Nasdaq DJT, exploring the major milestones, booms, and busts that have defined its journey. Through detailed examples, we aim to provide a comprehensive understanding of how the DJT has performed over time, offering critical lessons for investors and analysts alike.

The Early Years: Foundation and Growth

The Dow Jones Transportation Average was established in 1884 by Charles Dow, who also co-founded Dow Jones & Company and The Wall Street Journal. The DJT was initially composed of nine railroad companies and two non-railroad companies, reflecting the dominance of railroads in the transportation sector during that era. Railroads were the primary means of moving goods across the expanding United States, supporting economic growth through the rapid industrialization and westward expansion of the late 19th century. The early years of the DJT were marked by the rapid growth of the railroad industry, which played a pivotal role in shaping the U.S. economy.

Example: During the late 19th century, the completion of the Transcontinental Railroad in 1869 significantly boosted the railroad industry, leading to an economic boom in the transportation sector. The inclusion of major railroads in the DJT, such as Union Pacific and Central Pacific, reflected the importance of these companies in the American economy. As the rail network expanded, these companies saw their stock prices rise, contributing to the overall growth of the DJT. This period highlighted the strong correlation between infrastructure development and the transportation sector's performance. The expansion of the railroad network facilitated the movement of raw materials to factories and finished goods to markets, fueling industrial growth and increasing economic activity across the country.

Example: The Panic of 1893, a severe economic depression, had a profound impact on the transportation sector, particularly the railroads. The collapse of several major railroads due to overexpansion and mismanagement led to a sharp decline in the DJT, demonstrating the index's sensitivity to financial crises. This downturn marked one of the earliest examples of how economic instability could directly affect the transportation sector, setting a precedent for future market cycles. The Panic of 1893 also underscored the risks associated with rapid expansion and the importance of prudent financial management in the transportation industry.

Example: The role of railroads in the industrialization of the United States cannot be overstated. By the late 19th century, railroads had connected remote agricultural regions with major industrial centers, enabling the efficient transport of goods and raw materials. The economic impact of this connectivity was profound, as it allowed industries to scale up production, reduce costs, and reach broader markets. The DJT's early performance, driven largely by railroad stocks, reflected the critical role these companies played in the economic expansion of the period. However, this dependence on railroads also made the DJT vulnerable to the boom-and-bust cycles that characterized the railroad industry during this era.

The Roaring Twenties and the Great Depression

The 1920s, often referred to as the "Roaring Twenties," were a period of significant economic growth and industrial expansion in the United States. The transportation sector, particularly railroads, continued to play a critical role in supporting this growth. However, the decade also saw the emergence of new transportation technologies, such as automobiles and airplanes, which began to challenge the dominance of railroads. The DJT started to evolve during this period, reflecting the broader changes taking place within the transportation sector.

Example: The introduction of the Model T by Ford in 1908 revolutionized the automotive industry, leading to the widespread adoption of automobiles. By the 1920s, the growing popularity of cars and trucks started to impact the railroad industry, as more goods were transported by road. This shift was reflected in the DJT, which began to include trucking companies and other non-railroad transportation firms to better represent the evolving industry. The diversification of the DJT during this period marked the beginning of its transition from a railroad-focused index to one that encompassed the broader transportation sector. The rise of the automobile industry also spurred the development of new infrastructure, such as highways and bridges, further reducing the reliance on railroads and driving the growth of the trucking industry.

Example: The stock market crash of 1929 and the subsequent Great Depression had a devastating impact on the transportation sector. As the economy contracted, demand for transportation services plummeted, leading to widespread bankruptcies and financial difficulties for many transportation companies. The DJT experienced a significant decline, reflecting the severe downturn in the sector. For instance, railroad companies, which had heavily invested in expanding their networks during the 1920s, faced declining revenues and mounting debts. The Great Depression underscored the vulnerability of the transportation sector to economic shocks and highlighted the DJT's role as an early indicator of broader economic distress. The contraction of the transportation sector during the Great Depression also led to significant job losses and a slowdown in industrial production, further exacerbating the economic downturn.

Example: During the Roaring Twenties, the rise of air travel also began to influence the transportation sector. Although still in its infancy, the airline industry started to gain traction as a viable means of passenger and cargo transport. Companies like Boeing and Curtiss-Wright began developing aircraft that could travel longer distances and carry more passengers, setting the stage for the rapid growth of commercial aviation in the decades to come. The inclusion of early airline stocks in the DJT marked the beginning of a new era in transportation, as the index expanded to reflect the diversification of the industry. This period also saw the emergence of air freight services, which offered faster delivery options for high-value and time-sensitive goods, further diversifying the transportation sector.

Post-War Boom and the Rise of Air Travel

The period following World War II was marked by a massive economic expansion, often referred to as the "post-war boom." This era saw significant investments in infrastructure, technological advancements, and the rise of new transportation modes, particularly air travel. The DJT, reflecting these changes, evolved to include a broader range of transportation companies, capturing the growth of airlines, trucking firms, and logistics companies.

Example: The introduction of commercial jet airliners in the 1950s, such as the Boeing 707, revolutionized air travel, making it faster, more efficient, and more accessible to the public. The rapid growth of the airline industry during this period was reflected in the DJT, which began to include major airlines such as American Airlines and Pan American World Airways. The expansion of air travel not only boosted the DJT but also signaled a shift in consumer preferences from rail to air travel, especially for long-distance trips. This period also saw the growth of cargo airlines, which played an increasingly important role in global trade, further diversifying the DJT's composition. The development of jet engines, which offered greater speed and fuel efficiency, also contributed to the growth of the airline industry and its impact on the DJT.

Example: The construction of the Interstate Highway System in the United States, initiated in 1956, had a profound impact on the trucking industry. The improved road network facilitated the efficient movement of goods by truck, leading to the expansion of the trucking sector. Companies like J.B. Hunt and Schneider National, which later became components of the DJT, benefited from the increased demand for road freight services. This development underscored the importance of infrastructure investments in driving the growth of the transportation sector and shaping the DJT's trajectory. The Interstate Highway System also contributed to the rise of suburbanization, as people moved away from urban centers, increasing the demand for transportation services to connect these new communities with employment centers and markets.

Example: The post-war boom also saw the expansion of international trade, which played a critical role in driving the growth of the transportation sector. The establishment of the Bretton Woods system and the General Agreement on Tariffs and Trade (GATT) created a more stable and open global trading environment, leading to increased demand for shipping and logistics services. The DJT benefited from these trends, as companies involved in international trade, such as shipping lines and freight forwarders, became increasingly important components of the index. The growth of containerization, which standardized the packaging and transport of goods, further boosted the efficiency of global trade and the transportation sector's performance.

THE OIL CRISES OF THE 1970S

The 1970s were a tumultuous decade for the transportation sector, marked by the oil crises of 1973 and 1979. These events had a significant impact on the DJT, as rising fuel prices led to increased operational costs for transportation companies, squeezing profit margins and reducing demand for services. The oil crises underscored the transportation sector's vulnerability to energy price shocks and highlighted the need for greater fuel efficiency and alternative energy sources.

Example: The 1973 oil embargo, initiated by the Organization of Arab Petroleum Exporting Countries (OAPEC), led to a dramatic increase in oil prices, which severely impacted the transportation sector. Airlines, in particular, were hard hit, as fuel costs accounted for a large portion of their expenses. Many airlines were forced to raise ticket prices, reduce capacity, and even ground less fuel-efficient aircraft. The DJT reflected these challenges, with airline stocks experiencing sharp declines. Similarly, trucking companies faced increased fuel costs, which they struggled to pass on to customers due to competitive pressures. The oil crisis highlighted the vulnerability of the transportation sector to energy price shocks and demonstrated the DJT's sensitivity to external economic factors. The crisis also prompted airlines to explore new technologies and operational strategies to improve fuel efficiency, such as the development of more aerodynamic aircraft designs and the implementation of fuel hedging practices.

Example: The 1979 oil crisis, triggered by the Iranian Revolution, further exacerbated the challenges facing the transportation sector. Once again, rising fuel prices led to higher operational costs for airlines, trucking companies, and shipping firms. The DJT experienced significant volatility during this period, with sharp declines in response to the escalating crisis. However, the crisis also spurred innovations in fuel efficiency and the development of alternative energy sources, leading some transportation companies to invest in more fuel-efficient technologies. For instance, airlines began exploring new aircraft designs that offered better fuel efficiency, while trucking companies invested in more efficient engines and aerodynamic truck designs. The development of fuel-efficient technologies, such as the Boeing 767 and the introduction of lightweight materials in aircraft construction, also helped mitigate the impact of high fuel prices on the transportation sector.

Example: The oil crises of the 1970s also had a lasting impact on consumer behavior and transportation demand. The sharp rise in fuel prices led to a shift in consumer preferences towards more fuel-efficient vehicles, such as compact cars and hybrids. This shift reduced the demand for larger, less fuel-efficient vehicles, which in turn affected the automotive and trucking industries. The DJT, reflecting these changes, experienced volatility as transportation companies adjusted to the new market dynamics. The crises also highlighted the importance of energy independence and the need for investments in alternative energy sources, such as natural gas, solar power, and electric vehicles.

The Deregulation Era

The late 1970s and early 1980s saw significant deregulation of the transportation sector, particularly in the United States. The deregulation of airlines, railroads, and trucking fundamentally changed the competitive landscape, leading to increased competition, lower prices, and significant industry consolidation. The DJT, reflecting these changes, experienced considerable shifts as companies adapted to the new regulatory environment.

Example: The Airline Deregulation Act of 1978 in the United States marked the beginning of a new era for the airline industry. Prior to deregulation, the government tightly controlled airline routes, fares, and schedules. Deregulation removed these controls, allowing airlines to set their own prices and routes, leading to increased competition. This period saw the emergence of new low-cost carriers, such as Southwest Airlines, which capitalized on the opportunity to offer lower fares and more flexible services. The increased competition drove down airfares, making air travel more accessible to the public. However, deregulation also led to financial instability for many airlines, resulting in bankruptcies and mergers. The DJT reflected these industry changes, with significant volatility in airline stocks as the market adjusted to the new competitive landscape. The emergence of hub-and-spoke systems, where airlines concentrated their operations at major hubs and connected them with smaller spokes, also played a key role in shaping the post-deregulation airline industry.

Example: The Staggers Rail Act of 1980 similarly deregulated the railroad industry, allowing railroads greater flexibility in setting rates and service terms. This deregulation led to increased competition among railroads, improved efficiency, and the ability to offer more customized services to shippers. The act also facilitated the consolidation of the railroad industry, with several mergers and acquisitions leading to the formation of larger, more efficient rail networks. The DJT benefited from the improved profitability of the railroad companies, which became leaner and more competitive in the post-deregulation era. The increased flexibility in pricing and service offerings allowed railroads to better compete with other modes of transportation, such as trucking and air freight, further strengthening the industry.

Example: The deregulation of the trucking industry, initiated by the Motor Carrier Act of 1980, also had a profound impact on the transportation sector. The act reduced the regulatory barriers to entry for new trucking companies, leading to increased competition and lower freight rates. While this benefited shippers by reducing transportation costs, it also led to consolidation within the industry, as smaller trucking firms struggled to compete with larger, more efficient operators. The DJT reflected these changes, with increased volatility in trucking stocks as the industry adjusted to the new competitive environment. The rise of third-party logistics providers (3PLs) during this period also played a significant role in shaping the post-deregulation transportation landscape, as these companies offered shippers a range of services, including freight brokerage, warehousing, and supply chain management.

The Technology Boom and Globalization

The late 20th and early 21st centuries were characterized by rapid technological advancements and the rise of globalization. These trends had a profound impact on the transportation sector, driving growth and innovation across all modes of transport. The DJT, which had already diversified to include a broad range of transportation companies, continued to evolve in response to these changes.

Example: The rise of the internet and e-commerce in the 1990s transformed the logistics and shipping industries. Companies like FedEx and UPS, which had already established themselves as leaders in express delivery services, expanded their operations to meet the growing demand for online shopping. The advent of just-in-time delivery models and sophisticated tracking systems allowed these companies to offer faster, more reliable services, further boosting their growth. The DJT reflected the success of these companies, with FedEx and UPS becoming key components of the index. The technology boom also facilitated the growth of global supply chains, with transportation companies playing a critical role in connecting manufacturers with consumers around the world. The development of advanced logistics software and data analytics tools also enabled transportation companies to optimize their operations, reducing costs and improving service levels.

Example: The globalization of trade during this period also spurred significant growth in the shipping industry. As global trade volumes increased, shipping companies invested in larger, more efficient vessels to meet the demand for international freight services. The expansion of global trade agreements, such as the North American Free Trade Agreement (NAFTA) and the World Trade Organization (WTO), further boosted the transportation sector by reducing trade barriers and increasing the flow of goods across borders. The DJT benefited from these trends, with shipping and logistics companies experiencing strong growth as they expanded their global operations. The development of intermodal transportation, which combines multiple modes of transport (such as rail, truck, and ship) to move goods more efficiently, also played a key role in the growth of global trade and the transportation sector.

Example: The rise of containerization revolutionized the shipping industry by standardizing the packaging and transport of goods. The use of standardized containers allowed for more efficient loading and unloading of ships, reducing port turnaround times and lowering transportation costs. This innovation played a critical role in the growth of global trade, as it enabled the seamless movement of goods across different modes of transport, including ships, trains, and trucks. The DJT, which includes major shipping companies, reflected the positive impact of containerization on the transportation sector, as companies that embraced this technology saw significant improvements in efficiency and profitability.

The Financial Crisis of 2008

The global financial crisis of 2008 was one of the most significant economic events of the 21st century, with far-reaching impacts on the transportation sector. The crisis led to a sharp contraction in global trade, reduced consumer demand, and widespread financial instability. The DJT, reflecting these challenges, experienced significant declines as transportation companies struggled to navigate the downturn.

Example: The collapse of Lehman Brothers in September 2008 triggered a global financial panic, leading to a severe contraction in economic activity. As businesses cut back on production and consumers reduced spending, demand for transportation services plummeted. The DJT, which had already been declining in response to the slowing economy, saw sharp drops as the crisis deepened. Airlines, which rely heavily on business and leisure travel, were particularly hard hit, with many carriers facing financial difficulties. For example, Delta Air Lines and American Airlines both reported significant losses during this period, leading to layoffs, route reductions, and cost-cutting measures. The financial crisis also led to a wave of bankruptcies and consolidations in the airline industry, as carriers struggled to survive the sharp decline in demand.

Example: The shipping industry also faced significant challenges during the financial crisis. As global trade volumes collapsed, shipping companies were left with excess capacity and declining freight rates. The Baltic Dry Index, a key measure of global shipping costs, plummeted by more than 90% from its peak in 2008, reflecting the steep decline in demand for bulk shipping. Shipping companies like Maersk and Hanjin Shipping faced financial difficulties, with some smaller operators going bankrupt. The DJT, which includes several major shipping and logistics companies, reflected the turmoil in the industry, with significant declines in shipping-related stocks. The crisis also highlighted the vulnerabilities in global supply chains, as companies struggled to manage the disruptions caused by the collapse in trade and financial markets.

Example: The financial crisis also had a significant impact on the railroad industry. As industrial production declined and consumer demand weakened, the volume of goods transported by rail decreased sharply. This led to a decline in revenue for railroad companies, which had to cut costs and reduce capacity to cope with the downturn. The DJT reflected these challenges, with railroad stocks experiencing significant declines during the crisis. However, the railroad industry also demonstrated resilience, as companies focused on improving operational efficiency and optimizing their networks to weather the storm. The recovery of the railroad industry in the years following the crisis underscored the importance of adaptability and strategic planning in navigating economic downturns.

Recovery and the Impact of E-Commerce

The period following the financial crisis saw a gradual recovery in the global economy, with the transportation sector playing a critical role in supporting the rebound. The rise of e-commerce, in particular, emerged as a key driver of growth for the transportation industry, leading to significant changes in the composition and performance of the DJT.

Example: The recovery of the global economy after the financial crisis was supported by a resurgence in consumer spending and industrial production. As businesses ramped up production to meet growing demand, the transportation sector saw increased activity across all modes of transport. The DJT, which had been severely impacted by the crisis, began to recover as transportation companies reported improved earnings. The rise of e-commerce during this period played a particularly important role in driving growth for logistics and shipping companies. For instance, UPS and FedEx both expanded their operations to handle the growing volume of online orders, investing in new technologies and infrastructure to improve delivery efficiency. The success of these companies was reflected in the DJT, which saw strong gains in logistics-related stocks. The growth of e-commerce also spurred innovation in delivery services, such as the development of drone delivery systems and the use of artificial intelligence to optimize delivery routes.

Example: The expansion of global supply chains during the post-crisis recovery also contributed to the growth of the transportation sector. As businesses sought to reduce costs and improve efficiency, they increasingly turned to global sourcing and just-in-time delivery models. This shift required more sophisticated logistics networks, with transportation companies playing a key role in managing the flow of goods across borders. The DJT benefited from the increased demand for transportation services, particularly in the shipping and logistics sectors. Companies like Maersk and DHL expanded their global operations, taking advantage of the growing demand for international freight services. The development of advanced supply chain management systems, which use data analytics and real-time tracking to optimize the movement of goods, also played a key role in the growth of global trade and the transportation sector.

Example: The rise of e-commerce also led to the growth of new business models in the transportation sector. For example, the gig economy has given rise to companies like Uber and Lyft, which have disrupted the traditional taxi and delivery industries by offering flexible, on-demand services. The DJT, reflecting these changes, has adapted to include companies involved in these emerging business models, highlighting the index's ability to evolve in response to changes in the transportation sector. The growth of ride-sharing and delivery services has also spurred innovation in vehicle technology, such as the development of electric and autonomous vehicles, which have the potential to further transform the transportation landscape.

The COVID-19 Pandemic

The COVID-19 pandemic, which began in late 2019, had an unprecedented impact on the global economy and the transportation sector. The pandemic led to widespread travel restrictions, disruptions in global supply chains, and significant changes in consumer behavior. The DJT, reflecting the turmoil in the transportation sector, experienced significant volatility during this period.

Example: The airline industry was one of the hardest hit by the pandemic, with global air travel coming to a near standstill in early 2020. Airlines faced a sharp decline in passenger numbers as governments imposed travel bans and consumers canceled trips due to health concerns. Many airlines were forced to ground large portions of their fleets, lay off employees, and seek government bailouts to survive the crisis. The DJT, which includes several major airlines, reflected the severe downturn in the industry, with airline stocks experiencing sharp declines. For example, Delta Air Lines and United Airlines both reported significant losses in 2020, leading to widespread cost-cutting measures and restructuring efforts. The pandemic also accelerated the adoption of digital technologies in the airline industry, such as contactless check-in and biometric screening, as airlines sought to reassure passengers and improve safety measures.

Example: The pandemic also had a significant impact on global supply chains, leading to disruptions in the shipping and logistics sectors. As factories shut down and trade flows were disrupted, shipping companies faced delays, congestion, and increased costs. The DJT experienced significant volatility as investors reacted to the uncertainty surrounding global trade and the impact of the pandemic on transportation companies. However, the rise of e-commerce during the pandemic also provided a boost to logistics companies, as consumers increasingly turned to online shopping for their needs. Companies like UPS and FedEx saw increased demand for delivery services, leading to strong earnings growth and improved stock performance. The pandemic also highlighted the importance of supply chain resilience, as companies sought to diversify their suppliers and build more flexible logistics networks to cope with future disruptions.

Example: The COVID-19 pandemic also accelerated the adoption of contactless delivery and digital payment systems in the transportation sector. As consumers sought to minimize physical contact, companies like DoorDash and Instacart saw a surge in demand for their delivery services. The DJT, reflecting these changes, adapted to include companies involved in these new business models, highlighting the index's ability to evolve in response to changes in the transportation sector. The growth of contactless delivery services also spurred innovation in last-mile delivery, such as the use of robots and autonomous vehicles to reduce the need for human contact and improve delivery efficiency.

Technological Advancements and Future Outlook

Looking ahead, the transportation sector is poised to undergo significant changes driven by technological advancements, evolving consumer preferences, and the ongoing impact of globalization. The DJT, which has historically reflected the evolution of the transportation sector, is likely to continue adapting to these changes as new technologies and business models emerge.

Example: The development of autonomous vehicles, both in the trucking and passenger transport sectors, has the potential to revolutionize the transportation industry. Companies like Tesla and Waymo are leading the charge in developing self-driving technologies that could significantly reduce labor costs, increase safety, and improve efficiency. The widespread adoption of autonomous vehicles could lead to significant shifts in the DJT, as companies that successfully integrate these technologies into their operations gain a competitive edge. For example, logistics companies that adopt autonomous delivery trucks could see reduced costs and improved delivery times, boosting their profitability and stock performance. The development of advanced sensors and artificial intelligence systems, which enable autonomous vehicles to navigate complex environments and make real-time decisions, also plays a key role in the future of the transportation sector.

Example: The continued growth of e-commerce is also expected to drive further changes in the transportation sector. As consumers increasingly demand faster and more reliable delivery services, logistics companies will need to invest in new technologies and infrastructure to meet these expectations. The DJT is likely to benefit from the ongoing expansion of e-commerce, with logistics and shipping companies playing a central role in the sector's growth. Additionally, advancements in supply chain technology, such as blockchain and artificial intelligence, could further improve the efficiency and transparency of global logistics networks, leading to new opportunities for companies within the DJT. The integration of blockchain technology in supply chain management, for example, has the potential to enhance transparency and security by providing a decentralized and immutable record of transactions and shipments.

Example: The transportation sector is also likely to be influenced by the ongoing shift towards sustainability and environmental responsibility. As governments and consumers increasingly prioritize reducing carbon emissions, transportation companies will need to invest in cleaner technologies, such as electric vehicles and alternative fuels, to meet these demands. The DJT, reflecting these changes, may see increased representation of companies involved in sustainable transportation solutions. For instance, companies that develop electric or hydrogen-powered vehicles, or those that invest in renewable energy sources, could play a more prominent role in the index. The adoption of carbon-neutral shipping practices, such as the use of biofuels and wind-assisted propulsion, also represents a significant opportunity for the transportation sector to reduce its environmental impact and align with global sustainability goals.

Chapter 4: Key Components of the Nasdaq DJT

The Nasdaq DJT (Dow Jones Transportation Average) is a critical barometer of the transportation sector's health, composed of 20 leading companies that represent various industries within the sector. These companies span a wide range of transportation modes, including airlines, railroads, trucking, shipping, and logistics. Understanding the key components of the DJT is essential for investors who wish to gain insights into the transportation sector's dynamics and anticipate market trends. In this chapter, we will explore the major companies within the DJT, examining their roles, market influence, and how they interact with broader economic forces. Detailed examples will illustrate the significance of these companies in shaping the index's performance and, by extension, the transportation sector as a whole.

Airlines: Navigating Through Turbulence

The airline industry is a crucial component of the DJT, representing the sector that connects people and businesses across the globe through air travel. Airlines are highly sensitive to a variety of factors, including fuel prices, economic conditions, geopolitical events, and changes in consumer demand. The performance of airlines within the DJT can provide valuable insights into broader economic trends and the health of the global economy.

Example: Delta Air Lines, one of the largest and most prominent airlines in the DJT, plays a significant role in the index's performance. Delta's extensive network of domestic and international routes, coupled with its strong brand and customer loyalty, positions it as a major player in the global airline industry. However, Delta's performance is closely tied to external factors such as fuel prices and economic cycles. For instance, during periods of economic growth, Delta typically benefits from increased demand for both business and leisure travel, leading to higher revenues and profitability. Conversely, during economic downturns, such as the Great Recession of 2008 or the COVID-19 pandemic, Delta faced sharp declines in passenger numbers, resulting in significant financial challenges. The airline's response to these challenges, such as implementing cost-cutting measures, renegotiating contracts, and seeking government assistance, has a direct impact on the DJT's overall performance.

Example: Southwest Airlines, another major airline in the DJT, is known for its low-cost business model and strong operational efficiency. Southwest's focus on point-to-point routes and its use of a single aircraft type (the Boeing 737) have allowed it to maintain low operating costs and offer competitive fares. This business model has made Southwest one of the most profitable airlines in the industry, even during periods of economic turbulence. For example, during the 2008 financial crisis, Southwest was able to maintain profitability by hedging fuel costs and leveraging its low-cost structure. This resilience contributed to the stability of the DJT, as Southwest's strong performance helped offset declines in other airline stocks within the index.

Example: The airline industry's exposure to geopolitical risks is another important factor that influences the DJT. For instance, American Airlines, a major component of the DJT, has been significantly impacted by geopolitical events such as the Gulf War, the 9/11 terrorist attacks, and the subsequent wars in Iraq and

Afghanistan. These events led to sharp declines in air travel demand, increased security costs, and disruptions in global operations. The impact of these geopolitical risks on American Airlines, and by extension the DJT, underscores the importance of understanding the broader geopolitical landscape when analyzing the transportation sector.

RAILROADS: THE BACKBONE OF FREIGHT TRANSPORTATION

Railroads are a critical component of the transportation sector, responsible for moving bulk goods such as coal, agricultural products, and industrial materials over long distances. The inclusion of major railroad companies in the DJT reflects the importance of this industry in supporting economic growth and industrial production. Railroads are also capital-intensive, requiring significant investments in infrastructure, equipment, and maintenance.

Example: Union Pacific, one of the largest railroad companies in the United States and a key component of the DJT, plays a vital role in transporting goods across the country. Union Pacific's extensive rail network connects major industrial centers, agricultural regions, and ports, making it a critical link in the supply chain. The company's performance is closely tied to the health of the U.S. economy, as demand for rail transport tends to increase during periods of economic expansion and decline during recessions. For instance, during the economic recovery following the 2008 financial crisis, Union Pacific benefited from increased demand for transporting agricultural products, construction materials, and consumer goods. This uptick in activity contributed to the DJT's recovery, as Union Pacific's strong performance bolstered the index.

Example: Norfolk Southern, another major railroad company in the DJT, is known for its focus on the eastern United States, where it operates a comprehensive rail network. Norfolk Southern plays a key role in transporting coal, automotive products, and intermodal freight, connecting manufacturers with markets across the country. The company's performance is influenced by a variety of factors, including changes in energy demand, shifts in manufacturing activity, and fluctuations in global trade. For example, the decline in coal consumption due to environmental regulations and the transition to cleaner energy sources has negatively impacted Norfolk Southern's coal transport business. However, the company has adapted by diversifying its freight mix and investing in intermodal transport, which has helped stabilize its revenue streams and maintain its position within the DJT.

Example: The railroad industry's ability to weather economic downturns and adapt to changing market conditions is a key factor in the DJT's stability. During periods of economic uncertainty, such as the 2020 COVID-19 pandemic, railroads like CSX Corporation demonstrated resilience by focusing on cost control, operational efficiency, and service reliability. CSX's efforts to streamline operations, optimize its rail network, and invest in technology allowed it to maintain profitability despite the challenges posed by the pandemic. This resilience contributed to the overall stability of the DJT, as railroads provided a steady foundation for the index during a volatile period.

Trucking: The Last-Mile Connection

The trucking industry is essential for the final leg of supply chains, delivering goods from warehouses to retail stores and directly to consumers. Trucking companies handle a significant portion of domestic freight, making them indispensable for the movement of goods across short and medium distances. The rise of e-commerce has further increased the demand for trucking services, particularly for last-mile delivery, where goods are transported from distribution centers to their final destinations.

Example: J.B. Hunt Transport Services, a leading trucking company and a key component of the DJT, plays a critical role in the U.S. transportation network. J.B. Hunt specializes in a variety of trucking services, including intermodal, dedicated contract services, and truckload transportation. The company's ability to offer a wide range of services has made it a preferred partner for many large retailers and manufacturers. For instance, the rise of e-commerce has led to increased demand for J.B. Hunt's intermodal services, which combine the efficiency of rail transport with the flexibility of trucking for the final delivery. This has allowed J.B. Hunt to capitalize on the growing need for efficient and reliable transportation solutions, contributing to the DJT's overall performance.

Example: The trucking industry's exposure to regulatory changes is another important factor that influences the DJT. For instance, the implementation of the Electronic Logging Device (ELD) mandate by the U.S. Federal Motor Carrier Safety Administration (FMCSA) in 2017 required trucking companies to install electronic devices that monitor the driving hours of truck drivers. This regulation aimed to improve road safety by ensuring compliance with hours-of-service rules. However, the mandate also led to increased costs for trucking companies, both in terms of purchasing and installing the devices and in the potential loss of productivity as drivers were forced to take longer rest periods. Smaller trucking companies, in particular, struggled with the financial burden of compliance, leading some to exit the industry altogether. The impact of the ELD mandate on the trucking industry, and by extension the DJT, highlights the importance of understanding regulatory changes when analyzing transportation stocks.

Example: The trucking industry's role in supporting the U.S. economy is also reflected in the performance of companies like Old Dominion Freight Line, another key component of the DJT. Old Dominion specializes in less-than-truckload (LTL) transportation, which involves the consolidation of multiple smaller shipments into a single truck. This business model has proven to be highly resilient, as it allows Old Dominion to serve a wide range of customers across various industries. For example, during periods of economic growth, Old Dominion benefits from increased demand for LTL services as manufacturers and retailers ramp up production and inventory levels. Conversely, during economic downturns, the company's ability to optimize routes, manage costs, and maintain service quality has helped it weather the storm, contributing to the DJT's stability.

SHIPPING AND LOGISTICS: THE ARTERIES OF GLOBAL TRADE

Shipping and logistics companies are the arteries of global trade, ensuring the smooth flow of goods across international borders. These companies manage complex supply chains, coordinating the movement of products from manufacturers to end consumers. The performance of shipping and logistics companies is closely tied to global trade volumes, making them sensitive to changes in trade policies, tariffs, and economic conditions.

Example: FedEx, a global logistics giant and a major component of the DJT, plays a critical role in connecting businesses and consumers around the world. FedEx offers a wide range of services, including express shipping, freight transportation, and supply chain management. The company's performance is closely tied to global trade volumes, as well as the growth of e-commerce. For instance, during the COVID-19 pandemic, FedEx experienced a surge in demand for its e-commerce and residential delivery services as consumers increasingly turned to online shopping. This surge in demand contributed to strong earnings growth for FedEx, which in turn supported the DJT's performance during a period of economic uncertainty.

Example: The impact of global trade tensions on shipping and logistics companies can be significant. For instance, during the U.S.-China trade war, companies like UPS faced increased uncertainty as tariffs and trade barriers disrupted supply chains. These disruptions often led to shifts in trade routes, delays, and increased costs, which were reflected in the financial performance of these companies and, by extension, in the DJT's overall performance. However, UPS's ability to adapt to these challenges, such as by diversifying its customer base and expanding its services in other regions, helped mitigate the impact of the trade war and maintain its position as a leading logistics provider.

Example: Maersk, one of the world's largest shipping companies and a key player in the DJT, is heavily influenced by global economic conditions and trade volumes. Maersk's performance is closely tied to the demand for container shipping, which is used to transport a wide range of goods across international borders. For example, during periods of economic expansion, Maersk typically benefits from increased demand for shipping services as global trade volumes rise. Conversely, during economic downturns, such as the 2008 financial crisis, Maersk faced challenges due to declining trade volumes and excess shipping capacity, which led to lower freight rates and reduced profitability. The company's ability to manage capacity, optimize operations, and invest in new technologies, such as digitalization and automation, has helped it navigate these challenges and maintain its position within the DJT.

INTERMODAL TRANSPORTATION: INTEGRATING MULTIPLE MODES

Intermodal transportation involves the use of multiple modes of transport, such as rail, truck, and ship, to move goods from origin to destination. This approach offers greater flexibility, efficiency, and cost-effectiveness compared to using a single mode of transport. Intermodal transportation has become increasingly important in the global supply chain, as it allows companies to optimize their logistics networks and reduce transportation costs.

Example: The role of intermodal transportation in the DJT is exemplified by companies like Kansas City Southern, a railroad company that also offers intermodal services. Kansas City Southern operates a network of rail lines that connect the United States with Mexico, facilitating the movement of goods across the border. The company's intermodal services allow it to transport goods more efficiently by combining rail and truck transport, reducing transit times and costs for customers. For example, during the expansion of the North American Free Trade Agreement (NAFTA), Kansas City Southern benefited from increased cross-border trade, which drove demand for its intermodal services. This growth contributed to the

DJT's performance, highlighting the importance of intermodal transportation in the modern logistics landscape.

Example: The integration of intermodal transportation into the logistics networks of companies like Schneider National, a leading trucking and logistics company, has also played a key role in the DJT's performance. Schneider National offers a range of intermodal services, including rail-truck combinations that allow customers to move goods more efficiently across long distances. The company's ability to leverage its extensive network of rail and truck partnerships has made it a preferred logistics provider for many large retailers and manufacturers. For instance, during peak shipping seasons, Schneider National's intermodal services help customers manage increased demand and avoid congestion at major ports and rail terminals, ensuring timely delivery of goods.

Example: Intermodal transportation's impact on global trade is also reflected in the performance of companies like CSX Corporation, a major railroad company in the DJT. CSX has invested heavily in intermodal terminals and infrastructure, enabling it to offer seamless rail-truck connections across its network. These investments have allowed CSX to capture a larger share of the intermodal market, particularly in the eastern United States, where demand for efficient and reliable transportation services is high. The growth of intermodal transportation has contributed to CSX's strong financial performance, which in turn has supported the DJT's overall stability.

LOGISTICS AND SUPPLY CHAIN MANAGEMENT: OPTIMIZING THE FLOW OF GOODS

Logistics and supply chain management companies play a critical role in optimizing the flow of goods from manufacturers to end consumers. These companies offer a wide range of services, including warehousing, inventory management, freight brokerage, and supply chain consulting. The performance of logistics companies in the DJT is closely tied to their ability to manage complex supply chains, adapt to changing market conditions, and leverage technology to improve efficiency.

Example: Expeditors International, a global logistics company and a key component of the DJT, specializes in freight forwarding, customs brokerage, and supply chain management services. Expeditors' ability to navigate complex international trade regulations and manage the flow of goods across borders has made it a preferred partner for many multinational companies. For example, during the COVID-19 pandemic, Expeditors played a critical role in managing supply chain disruptions by offering flexible logistics solutions, such as air charter services and alternative shipping routes. The company's ability to adapt to these challenges and maintain service levels contributed to its strong financial performance, which supported the DJT during a period of global uncertainty.

Example: The rise of e-commerce has also driven demand for advanced logistics solutions, as companies seek to meet the growing expectations of online shoppers. Companies like C.H. Robinson, a leading logistics provider in the DJT, have invested in technology and data analytics to optimize their supply chain operations and offer more efficient and cost-effective services. For instance, C.H. Robinson's digital platforms allow customers to track shipments in real-time, manage inventory levels, and optimize delivery routes, reducing costs and improving service levels. The company's ability to leverage technology to enhance its logistics services has been a key driver of its success, contributing to the DJT's overall performance.

Example: The importance of supply chain resilience and flexibility is also reflected in the performance of companies like Ryder System, a leading provider of supply chain, transportation, and fleet management solutions. Ryder's ability to offer end-to-end logistics services, including warehousing, transportation, and fleet leasing, has made it a trusted partner for many large companies. For example, during periods of economic uncertainty, such as the 2008 financial crisis and the COVID-19 pandemic, Ryder's ability to offer flexible logistics solutions, such as temporary warehousing and on-demand transportation, helped its customers manage disruptions and maintain business continuity. The company's strong performance during these periods has supported the DJT's stability, highlighting the importance of supply chain management in the transportation sector.

Chapter 5: Economic Forces Influencing the Nasdaq DJT

The Nasdaq DJT (Dow Jones Transportation Average) is deeply intertwined with the broader economic forces that shape the global transportation sector. Understanding these forces is crucial for investors, analysts, and anyone interested in the dynamics of the DJT. The transportation sector is not isolated; it reacts to and influences a wide array of economic variables, such as fuel prices, interest rates, global trade policies, technological advancements, and consumer demand. Each of these factors can significantly impact the companies within the DJT, thereby affecting the overall performance of the index. This chapter delves into these key economic forces, providing detailed examples to illustrate their effects on the transportation sector and the DJT.

Fuel Prices: The Lifeblood of Transportation

Fuel is one of the most significant operational costs for transportation companies, making the sector highly sensitive to fluctuations in fuel prices. Whether it's jet fuel for airlines, diesel for trucks, or bunker fuel for ships, changes in fuel prices can have a profound impact on the profitability of transportation companies and, by extension, the DJT.

Example: The 2008 oil price spike is a critical case study in understanding the impact of fuel prices on the transportation sector. In mid-2008, oil prices surged to over $140 per barrel, driven by increased global demand and geopolitical tensions. For airlines like American Airlines and Delta Air Lines, both major components of the DJT, the sharp rise in fuel costs led to a dramatic increase in operating expenses. As a result, airlines were forced to implement fuel surcharges, reduce capacity, and even ground older, less fuel-efficient aircraft. These measures, while necessary to manage costs, had the unintended effect of reducing service availability and customer satisfaction, leading to a decline in ticket sales. The high fuel costs squeezed profit margins, leading to significant declines in airline stock prices and contributing to the overall downturn of the DJT during this period.

Example: The trucking industry, represented in the DJT by companies like J.B. Hunt Transport Services and Old Dominion Freight Line, also felt the impact of rising fuel prices in 2008. Trucking companies, which rely heavily on diesel fuel, faced skyrocketing operating costs. Unlike airlines, trucking companies could not easily pass these costs on to customers due to intense competition and long-term contracts that locked in freight rates. Many smaller trucking firms, unable to absorb the increased costs, were forced to shut down or merge with larger operators. However, companies like J.B. Hunt managed to navigate the crisis by improving fuel efficiency through better route planning, investing in more fuel-efficient trucks, and implementing fuel surcharges where possible. These strategies helped mitigate the impact of high fuel prices on their profitability, but the overall effect on the DJT was still negative, as the sector as a whole suffered from reduced profit margins and lower stock prices.

Example: Conversely, the sharp drop in oil prices in 2014 had a positive impact on the transportation sector and the DJT. As oil prices fell from over $100 per barrel to below $50 per barrel, transportation companies across the board saw a significant reduction in fuel costs. Airlines, in particular, benefited from the lower fuel prices, which boosted their profit margins and led to a surge in stock prices. Delta Air Lines, for example, reported a substantial increase in profitability in 2015 due to the savings on fuel, which in turn contributed to the overall rise in the DJT. The trucking industry also benefited from lower fuel prices, with companies like Old Dominion Freight Line seeing improved profit margins and increased demand for their services as lower fuel costs made transportation more affordable for customers. This period underscored the volatility of the transportation sector in response to fuel price fluctuations and highlighted the importance of strategic fuel management.

Interest Rates: The Cost of Capital

Interest rates are a crucial economic factor that affects the transportation sector, influencing everything from borrowing costs to consumer demand. Changes in interest rates, driven by central bank policies, can have both direct and indirect effects on the companies within the DJT and their stock prices.

Example: The Federal Reserve's interest rate hikes in the mid-2000s provide a clear example of how rising interest rates can impact the transportation sector. As the Fed raised rates to combat inflation, the cost of borrowing increased for companies across the transportation sector. For capital-intensive industries like railroads and airlines, represented in the DJT by companies like Union Pacific and Southwest Airlines, higher interest rates meant higher costs for financing new infrastructure, aircraft, and equipment. This increase in capital costs put pressure on profit margins and led to reduced investment in expansion projects. Additionally, higher interest rates tend to dampen consumer spending, which can lead to lower demand for transportation services, further impacting the DJT's performance. The combined effect of higher borrowing costs and reduced consumer demand created a challenging environment for transportation companies, resulting in a more volatile DJT during this period.

Example: The impact of interest rates on consumer spending is particularly evident in the airline industry. When interest rates rise, consumers face higher borrowing costs for credit cards, mortgages, and other loans, which can lead to a reduction in discretionary spending, including travel. For airlines like American Airlines, higher interest rates can translate into lower passenger numbers, reduced revenues, and downward pressure on stock prices. This relationship between interest rates and consumer demand is a critical factor that investors must consider when analyzing the DJT, as changes in interest rates can have a ripple effect across the entire transportation sector. For example, during periods of high interest rates, consumers may opt for cheaper travel alternatives, such as driving or using public transportation, rather than flying, further exacerbating the impact on airline revenues and the DJT.

Example: Conversely, periods of low interest rates can provide a boost to the transportation sector by lowering borrowing costs and stimulating consumer spending. For instance, in the aftermath of the 2008 financial crisis, the Federal Reserve implemented a series of rate cuts to stimulate the economy. The resulting low interest rates made it cheaper for transportation companies to finance new projects and expand their operations. Railroads like Norfolk Southern took advantage of these lower borrowing costs to invest in infrastructure upgrades and fleet expansion, which positioned them for growth as the economy recovered. Additionally, the low interest rates helped boost consumer spending, leading to increased demand for transportation services and contributing to the DJT's recovery. The combination of lower capital costs and increased consumer demand created a favorable environment for transportation companies, leading to stronger performance across the DJT.

Global Trade Policies: Navigating Tariffs and Trade Agreements

The transportation sector is deeply intertwined with global trade, making it highly sensitive to changes in trade policies, tariffs, and international agreements. Shifts in trade dynamics can have a significant impact on the DJT, as they influence the flow of goods across borders and the demand for transportation services.

Example: The U.S.-China trade war, which began in 2018, had a profound impact on the transportation sector and the DJT. The imposition of tariffs on hundreds of billions of dollars' worth of goods led to a significant disruption in global supply chains, affecting companies across the DJT. Shipping companies like FedEx and UPS faced increased uncertainty as tariffs led to shifts in trade routes, delays, and higher costs for their customers. Additionally, the trade war caused a slowdown in global trade volumes, leading to excess capacity in the shipping industry and putting downward pressure on freight rates. The resulting decline in profitability for shipping companies was reflected in the DJT's performance, as the index experienced increased volatility during the trade war. The trade war also led to a shift in supply chain strategies, with many companies seeking to diversify their manufacturing bases and reduce reliance on Chinese suppliers, further complicating the logistics landscape.

Example: Railroads were also impacted by the U.S.-China trade war, particularly those involved in the transport of agricultural products and industrial goods. For instance, Union Pacific, which plays a key role in transporting U.S. agricultural exports to ports for shipment to China, faced challenges as tariffs on American soybeans, corn, and other products led to a sharp decline in export volumes. The reduction in agricultural exports resulted in lower demand for rail transport, which negatively impacted Union Pacific's revenue and contributed to the DJT's overall decline during the trade war. However, the company responded by diversifying its freight mix and exploring new markets, which helped mitigate some of the negative effects of the trade war on its business. Union Pacific's ability to adapt to changing trade dynamics highlights the resilience of well-managed transportation companies in navigating geopolitical challenges.

Example: On the other hand, trade agreements can have a positive impact on the transportation sector by increasing the flow of goods across borders and boosting demand for transportation services. The North American Free Trade Agreement (NAFTA), which went into effect in 1994, is a prime example of how trade agreements can benefit the DJT. NAFTA significantly increased trade between the United States, Canada, and Mexico, leading to a surge in cross-border transportation activity. Companies like Kansas City Southern, which operates a rail network connecting the U.S. with Mexico, saw increased demand for their services as a result of the agreement. The growth in cross-border trade contributed to the overall performance of the DJT, as transportation companies benefited from the increased flow of goods and the expansion of their operations. The success of NAFTA in stimulating trade and transportation activity underscores the importance of favorable trade policies in supporting the growth of the DJT and the broader transportation sector.

Example: The impact of Brexit on the transportation sector and the DJT serves as another example of how changes in trade policies can affect global trade dynamics. The United Kingdom's decision to leave the European Union created significant uncertainty for transportation companies involved in cross-border trade between the UK and EU member states. Companies like Maersk, a major player in the global shipping industry and a key component of the DJT, faced challenges related to changes in customs procedures, tariffs, and regulatory standards. The resulting disruptions in supply chains led to increased costs and delays, affecting the profitability of transportation companies. However, the adaptability of these companies in navigating the complexities of Brexit highlights the resilience of the transportation sector in the face of significant trade policy changes.

Technological Advancements: Driving Efficiency and Innovation

Technological advancements are a major driver of change in the transportation sector, influencing everything from operational efficiency to customer experience. The adoption of new technologies can have a significant impact on the companies within the DJT, offering both opportunities for growth and challenges related to implementation.

Example: The rise of e-commerce in the early 2000s revolutionized the logistics and shipping industries, creating new opportunities for companies like FedEx and UPS. The growing demand for fast and reliable delivery services led these companies to invest heavily in technology, such as advanced tracking systems, automated sorting facilities, and real-time inventory management. These investments allowed FedEx and UPS to meet the increasing expectations of e-commerce customers, resulting in significant revenue growth and strong stock performance. The success of these companies contributed to the overall rise of the DJT, highlighting the importance of technological innovation in the transportation sector. The ongoing development of technology-driven logistics solutions, such as drone delivery and autonomous vehicles, continues to shape the future of the transportation industry.

Example: The development of autonomous vehicles is another technological advancement with the potential to transform the transportation sector. Companies like Tesla and Waymo are leading the charge in developing self-driving trucks and cars, which promise to reduce labor costs, increase safety, and improve efficiency. For trucking companies like J.B. Hunt, the adoption of autonomous vehicles could lead to significant cost savings and operational improvements. However, the transition to autonomous vehicles also presents challenges, including regulatory hurdles, technological reliability, and potential job displacement for truck drivers. The impact of autonomous vehicles on the DJT will depend on how quickly and effectively companies within the index can adopt and integrate this technology into their operations. The potential for autonomous vehicles to disrupt the transportation sector underscores the importance of innovation and adaptability in maintaining competitiveness in a rapidly evolving industry.

Example: Technological advancements in the railroad industry, such as the implementation of Positive Train Control (PTC) systems, have also had a significant impact on the DJT. PTC is a safety system designed to prevent train collisions, derailments, and other accidents by automatically controlling train speeds and movements. The implementation of PTC across the U.S. rail network required significant investment from railroad companies like Norfolk Southern and Union Pacific. While the initial costs of implementing PTC were high, the long-term benefits of improved safety and operational efficiency have the potential to enhance the performance of these companies. The successful deployment of PTC and other technological innovations in the railroad industry has contributed to the stability and growth of the DJT. The ongoing integration of digital technologies, such as data analytics and predictive maintenance, further enhances the efficiency and reliability of railroad operations, positioning these companies for long-term success.

Consumer Demand: The Driving Force Behind Transportation

Consumer demand is a fundamental driver of the transportation sector, influencing everything from airline passenger numbers to the volume of goods shipped by truck or rail. Changes in consumer behavior, driven by factors such as economic conditions, technological advancements, and shifting preferences, can have a direct impact on the performance of transportation companies and the DJT.

Example: The rise of e-commerce has dramatically altered consumer expectations, leading to increased demand for fast and reliable delivery services. This shift has benefited logistics companies like UPS and FedEx, which have expanded their operations to meet the growing need for last-mile delivery. The growth of e-commerce has also led to increased demand for trucking services, particularly for companies like Old Dominion Freight Line that specialize in less-than-truckload (LTL) transportation. As more consumers shop online, the volume of small, frequent shipments has increased, driving demand for LTL services and contributing to the overall performance of the DJT. The continued expansion of e-commerce and the development of new delivery models, such as same-day delivery and click-and-collect services, are likely to drive further growth in the transportation sector.

Example: The airline industry's reliance on consumer demand for leisure and business travel is another key factor influencing the DJT. During periods of economic growth, consumers are more likely to spend on discretionary items such as vacations and travel, leading to increased passenger numbers and higher revenues for airlines. For example, in the years following the 2008 financial crisis, the gradual recovery of the global economy led to a resurgence in air travel demand, benefiting airlines like Delta Air Lines and contributing to the DJT's overall recovery. Conversely, during economic downturns, consumer demand for travel typically declines, leading to lower passenger numbers, reduced revenues, and downward pressure on airline stocks within the DJT. The cyclical nature of consumer demand in the airline industry highlights the importance of economic conditions in shaping the performance of transportation companies.

Example: Shifts in consumer preferences, such as the growing demand for environmentally friendly transportation options, can also influence the DJT. For instance, the increasing awareness of climate change and the desire to reduce carbon footprints have led to greater demand for electric vehicles and other sustainable transportation solutions. Companies like Tesla, which are at the forefront of the electric vehicle revolution, have benefited from this shift in consumer preferences. The adoption of electric vehicles has also influenced the trucking industry, with companies like J.B. Hunt exploring the use of electric trucks for short-haul and last-mile delivery services. The growing emphasis on sustainability in the transportation sector is likely to have a lasting impact on the DJT, as companies that successfully adapt to changing consumer preferences are likely to see strong performance. The development of green logistics solutions, such as carbon-neutral shipping and renewable energy-powered transportation, represents a significant opportunity for companies to align with consumer values and drive future growth.

Chapter 6: Investment Strategies for the Nasdaq DJT

The Nasdaq DJT (Dow Jones Transportation Average) offers a unique opportunity for investors to gain exposure to the transportation sector, a vital component of the global economy. However, investing in the DJT requires a nuanced understanding of the various strategies that can be employed to maximize returns while managing risk. This chapter will explore a range of investment strategies tailored to the DJT, including index funds, ETFs, sector rotation, and individual stock selection. By providing detailed examples, we will illustrate how these strategies can be effectively implemented to capitalize on the trends and opportunities within the transportation sector.

Index Funds and ETFs: Broad Exposure to the Transportation Sector

One of the most straightforward ways to invest in the Nasdaq DJT is through index funds and exchange-traded funds (ETFs). These investment vehicles offer broad exposure to the transportation sector by tracking the performance of the DJT as a whole. This approach allows investors to benefit from the overall growth of the sector without the need to pick individual stocks.

Example: The iShares Transportation Average ETF (IYT) is one of the most popular ETFs that tracks the Nasdaq DJT. By investing in IYT, investors gain exposure to all 20 companies within the DJT, including airlines, railroads, trucking firms, and logistics companies. This diversification helps to spread risk across multiple industries within the transportation sector, reducing the impact of poor performance by any single company. For instance, during the 2020 COVID-19 pandemic, while airlines like Delta Air Lines experienced significant declines due to reduced travel demand, logistics companies like FedEx saw increased demand for delivery services, which helped offset losses within the ETF. This balanced exposure allows investors to benefit from the broader trends within the transportation sector while minimizing the impact of sector-specific downturns.

Example: Another advantage of ETFs like IYT is their liquidity and ease of trading. Unlike mutual funds, which can only be traded at the end of the trading day, ETFs can be bought and sold throughout the trading day, allowing investors to react quickly to market developments. For instance, during the initial stages of the 2008 financial crisis, investors who held ETFs were able to quickly liquidate their positions as the DJT began to decline, potentially minimizing their losses. Additionally, ETFs typically have lower expense ratios compared to mutual funds, making them a cost-effective option for investors looking to gain exposure to the transportation sector.

Example: For long-term investors, index funds that track the DJT can be an effective way to benefit from the overall growth of the transportation sector. Over the past several decades, the DJT has experienced periods of significant growth, driven by factors such as globalization, technological advancements, and increased consumer demand for transportation services. By investing in an index fund, investors can capture these long-term trends without the need to constantly monitor and adjust their portfolios. For example, an investor who purchased shares in an index fund tracking the DJT in the early 2000s would have benefited from the subsequent growth of e-commerce and the corresponding increase in demand for logistics and delivery services, resulting in substantial capital appreciation over time.

SECTOR ROTATION: CAPITALIZING ON ECONOMIC CYCLES

Sector rotation is an investment strategy that involves shifting investments from one sector to another based on the expected performance of different sectors during various phases of the economic cycle. The transportation sector, as represented by the DJT, tends to be cyclical, meaning its performance is closely tied to the overall health of the economy. By understanding the economic cycle and the factors that drive the transportation sector, investors can use sector rotation to enhance their returns.

Example: During the early stages of an economic recovery, the transportation sector often experiences strong growth as consumer spending increases and businesses ramp up production. For instance, following the 2008 financial crisis, the U.S. economy began to recover in 2009, leading to increased demand for transportation services. Investors who anticipated this recovery and rotated into transportation stocks, such as those within the DJT, were able to capitalize on the subsequent growth. Companies like Union Pacific and FedEx saw significant increases in their stock prices as the economy rebounded and demand for freight and logistics services surged.

Example: Conversely, during the late stages of an economic expansion, the transportation sector may begin to show signs of slowing down as rising interest rates and inflation start to weigh on economic growth. In such scenarios, investors may choose to rotate out of transportation stocks and into more defensive sectors, such as utilities or consumer staples, which tend to perform better during economic downturns. For example, in the years leading up to the 2008 financial crisis, investors who recognized the signs of an impending economic slowdown and reduced their exposure to transportation stocks within the DJT were better positioned to weather the subsequent market downturn.

Example: Sector rotation can also be driven by specific events or developments within the transportation sector itself. For instance, during periods of rising fuel prices, airlines and trucking companies within the DJT may experience increased operating costs, leading to lower profit margins and declining stock prices. In such cases, investors may choose to rotate out of these stocks and into companies within the DJT that are less sensitive to fuel prices, such as railroads or logistics firms. By strategically rotating investments based on the specific conditions affecting the transportation sector, investors can potentially enhance their returns while managing risk.

Individual Stock Selection: Identifying Opportunities within the DJT

While investing in index funds or ETFs provides broad exposure to the transportation sector, some investors may prefer to take a more active approach by selecting individual stocks within the DJT. This strategy requires a deeper understanding of the companies within the index and the factors that drive their performance. By identifying opportunities within the DJT, investors can potentially achieve higher returns compared to a passive investment approach.

Example: One approach to individual stock selection within the DJT is to focus on companies with strong fundamentals, such as consistent revenue growth, solid profit margins, and a competitive advantage within their industry. For instance, FedEx is a company within the DJT that has consistently delivered strong financial performance due to its dominant position in the global logistics industry. The company's extensive network, advanced technology, and strong brand recognition have allowed it to maintain a competitive edge, even during periods of economic uncertainty. Investors who recognized FedEx's strong fundamentals and invested in the stock during periods of market volatility, such as the 2020 COVID-19 pandemic, were able to benefit from the subsequent recovery and growth in the company's stock price.

Example: Another approach is to identify companies within the DJT that are well-positioned to benefit from specific trends or developments within the transportation sector. For example, the growing demand for e-commerce has created significant opportunities for logistics companies like UPS, which is also a component of the DJT. As online shopping continues to grow, UPS has expanded its operations to meet the increasing demand for last-mile delivery services. Investors who recognized the potential of e-commerce and invested in UPS during the early stages of this trend have seen substantial gains in the stock's value as the company has capitalized on the growth of online retail.

Example: Some investors may also focus on turnaround opportunities within the DJT, identifying companies that are currently underperforming but have the potential for significant improvement. For instance, during periods of economic downturns or industry-specific challenges, certain companies within the DJT may experience temporary declines in their stock prices. However, if these companies have strong management teams, solid balance sheets, and a clear plan for addressing their challenges, they may be well-positioned for a recovery. Investors who can identify these turnaround opportunities and invest at the right time can potentially achieve significant returns as the company recovers and its stock price rebounds.

Dividend Investing: Generating Income from the DJT

Dividend investing is another strategy that can be applied to the DJT, particularly for investors seeking a steady stream of income. Many companies within the DJT, especially those in mature industries like railroads and logistics, pay regular dividends to their shareholders. By focusing on dividend-paying stocks within the DJT, investors can generate income while also benefiting from potential capital appreciation.

Example: Union Pacific, a leading railroad company within the DJT, is known for its consistent dividend payments and strong financial performance. The company has a long history of paying dividends, and it has consistently increased its dividend payout over time. For income-focused investors, Union Pacific offers an attractive combination of dividend yield and potential for capital appreciation. By investing in Union Pacific, investors can benefit from the company's stable cash flows, which are supported by its extensive rail network and strong market position, while also receiving regular dividend payments.

Example: Another dividend-paying stock within the DJT is UPS, which has also demonstrated a commitment to returning capital to shareholders through dividends. UPS's strong financial performance, driven by the growth of e-commerce and its dominant position in the logistics industry, has allowed the company to consistently pay and increase its dividends. For investors seeking both income and growth potential, UPS represents a compelling investment opportunity within the DJT.

Example: Dividend reinvestment is a strategy that can enhance the returns from dividend-paying stocks within the DJT. By reinvesting dividends to purchase additional shares, investors can benefit from the compounding effect, as the reinvested dividends generate additional dividends over time. For example, an investor who reinvests dividends from a stock like Norfolk Southern, another major railroad company within the DJT, can gradually increase their ownership stake in the company, leading to higher dividend income and potential capital gains in the long run.

Technical Analysis: Timing Entries and Exits in the DJT

Technical analysis is a strategy that involves using historical price data and chart patterns to predict future price movements. While fundamental analysis focuses on the intrinsic value of a company, technical analysis is concerned with market sentiment and the behavior of traders. By applying technical analysis to the DJT, investors can identify potential entry and exit points for their investments.

Example: One of the most common technical analysis tools is the moving average, which smooths out price data to identify trends.

For instance, a 50-day moving average can be used to track the short-term trend of a stock within the DJT. When the stock price crosses above its 50-day moving average, it is often seen as a bullish signal, indicating that the stock may be entering an uptrend. Conversely, when the stock price falls below its 50-day moving average, it may signal the beginning of a downtrend. Investors who use moving averages to time their entries and exits can potentially enhance their returns by aligning their investments with the prevailing market trend.

Example: Another technical analysis tool commonly used in the DJT is the Relative Strength Index (RSI), which measures the speed and change of price movements to identify overbought or oversold conditions. An RSI reading above 70 is typically considered overbought, suggesting that the stock may be due for a pullback, while an RSI reading below 30 is considered oversold, indicating that the stock may be undervalued. For example, if a stock within the DJT, such as Delta Air Lines, has an RSI reading above 70, an investor might consider selling or taking profits, anticipating a potential price correction. Conversely, if the RSI for a stock like J.B. Hunt falls below 30, it may present a buying opportunity, as the stock could be poised for a rebound.

Example: Chart patterns, such as head and shoulders, double tops, and triangles, are also commonly used in technical analysis to predict future price movements. For instance, a head and shoulders pattern, which consists of three peaks with the middle peak being the highest, is often seen as a bearish reversal signal. If a stock within the DJT, such as Norfolk Southern, forms a head and shoulders pattern, it may indicate that the stock is likely to decline in the near term. Investors who recognize these patterns can use them to inform their trading decisions, potentially improving their timing and enhancing their returns.

Chapter 7: Risk Management in Investing with the Nasdaq DJT

Investing in the Nasdaq DJT (Dow Jones Transportation Average) offers significant opportunities, but it also comes with various risks that investors must carefully manage. The transportation sector is subject to a wide range of risk factors, including economic downturns, volatility in fuel prices, regulatory changes, and geopolitical events. In this chapter, we will explore the key risks associated with investing in the DJT and discuss strategies for managing these risks effectively. Through detailed examples, we will illustrate how investors can mitigate potential losses and protect their portfolios while taking advantage of the growth opportunities in the transportation sector.

Market Risk: Navigating Economic Cycles

Market risk, or systematic risk, refers to the potential for an entire market or sector to decline in value due to economic conditions, geopolitical events, or other external factors. The transportation sector, as represented by the DJT, is particularly sensitive to economic cycles, with performance often tied closely to the overall health of the economy. Investors in the DJT must be aware of the potential for market risk and develop strategies to manage it.

Example: The 2008 financial crisis serves as a prime example of market risk impacting the DJT. As the global economy contracted, demand for transportation services plummeted, leading to sharp declines in the stock prices of companies within the DJT. Airlines like Delta Air Lines, which rely heavily on consumer spending and business travel, experienced significant losses as passengers cut back on travel expenses. Similarly, trucking and shipping companies faced reduced demand for freight services as businesses scaled back production and consumers reduced spending. Investors who were heavily exposed to the DJT during this period saw substantial declines in the value of their portfolios. However, those who diversified their investments across multiple sectors and asset classes were better able to weather the downturn and recover more quickly as the economy began to improve.

Example: To manage market risk, investors can employ strategies such as diversification and asset allocation. Diversification involves spreading investments across different sectors, industries, and asset classes to reduce the impact of a downturn in any single area. For instance, an investor with exposure to the DJT might also invest in defensive sectors like utilities or consumer staples, which tend to perform better during economic downturns. Additionally, asset allocation—adjusting the mix of stocks, bonds, and cash in a portfolio—can help manage market risk by balancing growth potential with stability. For example, during periods of economic uncertainty, an investor might increase their allocation to bonds and reduce their exposure to equities, including those within the DJT, to protect against potential losses.

Example: Another strategy for managing market risk is to use hedging techniques, such as options and futures contracts, to protect against adverse market movements. For instance, an investor holding a significant position in DJT-related stocks might purchase put options on the DJT or individual stocks within the index. These options provide the right to sell the stocks at a predetermined price, effectively setting a floor on potential losses. If the market declines, the value of the put options would increase, offsetting some of the losses in the underlying stocks. This approach can be particularly useful during periods of heightened market volatility or when economic indicators suggest a potential downturn.

Fuel Price Volatility: Managing Energy Costs

Fuel price volatility is a significant risk factor for the transportation sector, as fuel represents a major operational cost for companies within the DJT. Fluctuations in oil prices can have a direct impact on the profitability of airlines, trucking companies, and shipping firms, leading to increased volatility in their stock prices.

Example: The sharp increase in oil prices in 2008, when prices soared above $140 per barrel, had a severe impact on the transportation sector. Airlines like American Airlines and Southwest Airlines, which are heavily reliant on jet fuel, faced skyrocketing operating costs. As fuel expenses rose, these companies were forced to implement fuel surcharges, reduce capacity, and take other cost-cutting measures to preserve profitability. However, these measures were not enough to fully offset the impact of higher fuel prices, leading to significant declines in their stock prices and contributing to the overall downturn in the DJT. Investors who were heavily exposed to airline stocks during this period experienced substantial losses.

Example: To manage the risk of fuel price volatility, some transportation companies within the DJT use hedging strategies to lock in fuel prices and protect against price spikes. For example, Southwest Airlines has a long history of using fuel hedging to stabilize its fuel costs. By entering into contracts that fix the price of fuel for a specified period, Southwest has been able to mitigate the impact of rising fuel prices on its operating expenses. During periods of high oil prices, this strategy has provided Southwest with a competitive advantage over other airlines that did not hedge their fuel costs, allowing the company to maintain profitability and support its stock price. Investors who recognize the benefits of such hedging strategies may choose to invest in companies like Southwest that actively manage fuel price risk.

Example: Another approach to managing fuel price risk is to invest in companies within the DJT that are less sensitive to fuel price fluctuations. For instance, railroads like Union Pacific and Norfolk Southern, while still affected by fuel costs, tend to have more stable operating expenses compared to airlines and trucking companies. Railroads benefit from the efficiency of transporting large volumes of goods over long distances, which can offset the impact of higher fuel prices. Additionally, many railroads have fuel surcharge programs in place that allow them to pass on a portion of fuel cost increases to their customers, further stabilizing their revenue and profit margins. By including railroads in their portfolios, investors can reduce their exposure to fuel price volatility while still benefiting from the overall growth of the transportation sector.

Regulatory and Legal Risks: Navigating Compliance and Legislation

Regulatory and legal risks are another important consideration for investors in the DJT. The transportation sector is subject to a wide range of regulations, including environmental standards, safety requirements, and labor laws. Changes in these regulations can have significant implications for the companies within the DJT, affecting their operating costs, profitability, and overall market performance.

Example: The implementation of stricter emissions regulations, such as the International Maritime Organization's (IMO) 2020 sulfur cap, has had a major impact on the shipping industry. The IMO 2020 regulation requires ships to use fuel with a sulfur content of no more than 0.5%, down from the previous limit of 3.5%. This change has led to increased fuel costs for shipping companies, as compliant fuels are more expensive than traditional high-sulfur fuel. Companies like Maersk, one of the largest shipping companies in the world and a key component of the DJT, have had to invest in cleaner fuel technologies and retrofit their fleets to comply with the new regulations. These additional costs have squeezed profit margins and led to increased volatility in the stock prices of shipping companies. Investors who were aware of the impending regulatory changes and adjusted their portfolios accordingly were better positioned to manage this risk.

Example: Labor regulations and union negotiations can also pose significant risks for transportation companies within the DJT. For instance, the airline industry is heavily unionized, with pilots, flight attendants, and ground crew members often represented by powerful labor unions. Strikes, work stoppages, or protracted labor negotiations can lead to disruptions in operations, increased labor costs, and negative impacts on profitability. For example, in 2016, Delta Air Lines faced a potential strike by its pilots' union, which sought higher wages and better working conditions. The threat of a strike led to uncertainty in the market and a temporary decline in Delta's stock price as investors anticipated potential disruptions to the airline's operations. By monitoring labor relations and understanding the potential impact of labor disputes, investors can better manage the risks associated with labor-related issues in the DJT.

Example: Regulatory changes related to safety and environmental standards can also impact the profitability of transportation companies. For example, the Federal Aviation Administration (FAA) introduced new safety regulations in the wake of the 9/11 terrorist attacks, requiring airlines to implement enhanced security measures and make significant investments in airport security infrastructure. These regulations led to increased operating costs for airlines, which in turn affected their profit margins and stock prices. Similarly, trucking companies have faced increased regulatory scrutiny related to driver safety and hours-of-service rules, which limit the number of hours a driver can operate a commercial vehicle without rest. Compliance with these regulations requires investments in technology, such as electronic logging devices (ELDs), and can lead to reduced productivity, further impacting profitability. Investors who stay informed about regulatory developments and assess their potential impact on transportation companies can make more informed investment decisions and manage regulatory risk more effectively.

Geopolitical Risk: Navigating Global Uncertainty

Geopolitical risk refers to the potential for political events, such as wars, trade disputes, or changes in government policy, to impact the global economy and financial markets. The transportation sector is particularly vulnerable to geopolitical risk, as it is heavily reliant on global trade and the free movement of goods across borders. Geopolitical events can disrupt supply chains, increase costs, and create uncertainty in the market, all of which can negatively affect the DJT.

Example: The U.S.-China trade war, which began in 2018, is a prime example of geopolitical risk affecting the transportation sector. The imposition of tariffs on a wide range of goods disrupted global supply chains, leading to increased costs and uncertainty for companies within the DJT. Shipping companies like FedEx and UPS faced delays, rerouted shipments, and increased costs as they navigated the changing trade landscape. Additionally, the trade war led to a slowdown in global trade volumes, which negatively impacted the demand for transportation services and contributed to the overall volatility in the DJT. Investors who were aware of the potential impact of the trade war on the transportation sector and adjusted their portfolios accordingly were better able to manage this risk and protect their investments.

Example: Geopolitical events such as wars and conflicts can also have a significant impact on the transportation sector. For example, during the Gulf War in the early 1990s, oil prices surged as a result of supply disruptions in the Middle East. This increase in fuel costs led to higher operating expenses for airlines, trucking companies, and shipping firms, all of which are components of the DJT. The uncertainty surrounding the conflict and its potential impact on the global economy led to increased volatility in the stock prices of transportation companies. Investors who were heavily exposed to the DJT during this period experienced significant losses as the market reacted to the geopolitical uncertainty. To manage geopolitical risk, investors may choose to diversify their portfolios across different regions and sectors, reducing their reliance on any single market or industry.

Example: Another approach to managing geopolitical risk is to invest in companies within the DJT that have a strong global presence and diversified operations. For instance, Maersk, as a global shipping company, operates in multiple regions and serves a diverse customer base, which can help mitigate the impact of geopolitical events in any single market. Additionally, companies that have strong relationships with multiple governments and a track record of navigating complex regulatory environments may be better positioned to manage geopolitical risk. Investors who focus on companies with a global footprint and diversified operations can reduce their exposure to geopolitical risk while still benefiting from the growth of the transportation sector.

Company-Specific Risk: Evaluating Individual Stock Performance

Company-specific risk refers to the potential for an individual company's stock to decline in value due to factors unique to that company, such as poor management decisions, financial mismanagement, or operational challenges. When investing in the DJT, it is important for investors to evaluate the risks associated with each individual company and consider how these risks may impact the overall performance of their portfolios.

Example: The bankruptcy of Pacific Gas and Electric Company (PG&E) in 2019 serves as a cautionary tale of company-specific risk. While PG&E is not a component of the DJT, its experience highlights the importance of evaluating company-specific risk. PG&E's

financial troubles were largely due to its liability for devastating wildfires in California, which were linked to the company's equipment. The resulting legal liabilities and financial losses led to PG&E filing for bankruptcy, resulting in a significant decline in its stock price and losses for investors. Similarly, investors in the DJT must be vigilant in assessing the risks associated with individual companies, such as potential legal liabilities, operational challenges, or management decisions that could negatively impact their stock prices.

Example: In the transportation sector, company-specific risk can arise from a variety of factors, including operational inefficiencies, competitive pressures, and changes in consumer preferences. For example, in 2013, the airline industry was rocked by the bankruptcy of American Airlines, one of the largest carriers in the United States and a component of the DJT. American Airlines faced intense competition, high labor costs, and an outdated fleet, all of which contributed to its financial difficulties. The company's bankruptcy filing led to a significant decline in its stock price and losses for investors. However, those who conducted thorough due diligence and recognized the signs of financial distress were able to reduce their exposure to American Airlines before the bankruptcy, mitigating their losses.

Example: Another example of company-specific risk in the DJT is the performance of Tesla, a company that has been both a high-flyer and a source of significant volatility. Tesla's stock price has been influenced by a variety of factors, including production challenges, regulatory scrutiny, and CEO Elon Musk's public statements. While Tesla has delivered impressive growth and innovation in the electric vehicle market, it has also faced periods of significant volatility, driven by concerns about its financial stability and ability to meet production targets. Investors who closely monitored Tesla's financials and operational performance were better equipped to manage the risks associated with investing in such a volatile stock.

Example: To manage company-specific risk, investors can conduct thorough due diligence and analysis of each company within the DJT before making investment decisions. This analysis should include an assessment of the company's financial health, competitive position, management team, and potential risks. Additionally, investors can diversify their portfolios by investing in a range of companies within the DJT, rather than concentrating their investments in a single stock. By spreading their investments across multiple companies, investors can reduce the impact of poor performance by any one company on their overall portfolio.

Chapter 8: Understanding the Role of Macroeconomic Indicators in the Nasdaq DJT

Macroeconomic indicators are vital tools that investors use to assess the overall health of the economy and predict the future performance of financial markets, including the Nasdaq DJT (Dow Jones Transportation Average). The transportation sector, which is a cornerstone of economic activity, is particularly sensitive to these indicators. By understanding how macroeconomic indicators such as GDP growth, unemployment rates, consumer spending, inflation, and interest rates influence the DJT, investors can make more informed decisions and better manage their portfolios. In this chapter, we will explore the key macroeconomic indicators that impact the DJT, providing detailed explanations and numerous examples to illustrate their significance.

Gross Domestic Product (GDP) Growth: The Engine of Transportation Demand

Gross Domestic Product (GDP) growth is one of the most important macroeconomic indicators, as it measures the overall economic output of a country. The transportation sector, represented by the DJT, is closely linked to GDP growth because it relies on the movement of goods and people. When the economy is growing, businesses produce more goods, consumers spend more money, and demand for transportation services increases. Conversely, during periods of economic contraction, demand for transportation services tends to decline, negatively impacting the DJT.

Example: During the economic expansion of the mid-2000s, the U.S. economy experienced strong GDP growth, driven by robust consumer spending, industrial production, and a booming housing market. This period of growth led to increased demand for transportation services across various sectors. Airlines like Delta Air Lines and Southwest Airlines saw a surge in passenger numbers as both business and leisure travel increased. Similarly, trucking companies such as J.B. Hunt and Old Dominion Freight Line benefited from higher freight volumes as manufacturers ramped up production to meet rising consumer demand. The strong GDP growth during this period contributed to the overall rise of the DJT, as transportation companies experienced increased revenues and profitability.

Example: In contrast, the 2008 financial crisis led to a sharp contraction in GDP, with the U.S. economy entering a severe recession. As GDP declined, businesses cut back on production, consumers reduced spending, and demand for transportation services plummeted. Airlines, which are highly sensitive to changes in consumer and business spending, experienced significant declines in passenger numbers. Trucking and shipping companies faced reduced freight volumes as businesses scaled back operations and international trade slowed. The decline in GDP during the recession led to a sharp drop in the DJT, reflecting the negative impact of the economic downturn on the transportation sector.

Example: The COVID-19 pandemic in 2020 also provides a clear illustration of how GDP growth impacts the DJT. As the pandemic spread, governments around the world implemented lockdowns and travel restrictions, leading to a dramatic decline in economic activity. U.S. GDP contracted sharply in the second quarter of 2020, resulting in a significant decrease in demand for transportation services. Airlines were particularly hard hit, with many flights canceled and passenger numbers plummeting. Trucking companies faced disruptions in supply chains and reduced freight volumes. The contraction in GDP during the pandemic led to a significant decline in the DJT, as the transportation sector struggled to cope with the unprecedented economic challenges.

Unemployment Rates: A Barometer of Economic Health

The unemployment rate is a key indicator of labor market conditions and overall economic health. High unemployment rates typically signal economic distress, as businesses lay off workers and reduce hiring. Conversely, low unemployment rates indicate a strong labor market, with more people employed and earning income, which supports consumer spending and economic growth. The transportation sector, as reflected in the DJT, is directly impacted by changes in the unemployment rate.

Example: During the recovery from the 2008 financial crisis, the U.S. unemployment rate gradually declined as the economy began to stabilize. As more people found jobs, consumer confidence improved, leading to increased spending on goods and services. This, in turn, boosted demand for transportation services, particularly in the retail and logistics sectors. Companies like UPS and FedEx saw increased package volumes as e-commerce continued to grow, driven by rising consumer spending. The decline in the unemployment rate during the economic recovery contributed to the positive performance of the DJT, as transportation companies benefited from the improved labor market conditions.

Example: On the other hand, periods of rising unemployment can have a negative impact on the DJT. For example, during the early stages of the COVID-19 pandemic, the U.S. unemployment rate soared to its highest level since the Great Depression, as businesses across the country were forced to close or reduce operations. The sharp increase in unemployment led to a significant decline in consumer spending, particularly on discretionary items such as travel and entertainment. Airlines were among the hardest hit, with many flights grounded and revenue streams severely diminished. Trucking and shipping companies also faced challenges as businesses scaled back production and international trade slowed. The rise in unemployment during the pandemic contributed to the overall decline in the DJT, as the transportation sector struggled to navigate the economic downturn.

Example: The impact of unemployment on the DJT can also be seen in the labor-intensive nature of the transportation sector. For instance, the trucking industry, which relies heavily on a large workforce of drivers, is particularly sensitive to changes in labor market conditions. During periods of low unemployment, trucking companies may face challenges in recruiting and retaining drivers, leading to higher labor costs and potential disruptions in operations. Conversely, during periods of high unemployment, trucking companies may have access to a larger pool of available workers, which can help stabilize labor costs and support operational efficiency. Investors who monitor unemployment trends and their impact on the labor market within the transportation sector can gain valuable insights into the potential performance of the DJT.

Consumer Spending: The Fuel for Transportation Demand

Consumer spending is a critical driver of economic activity, accounting for a significant portion of GDP. The transportation sector is directly influenced by consumer spending patterns, as the movement of goods and people is closely tied to consumer demand. When consumers spend more, businesses produce more goods, and the demand for transportation services increases. Conversely, when consumer spending declines, demand for transportation services tends to fall, impacting the performance of the DJT.

Example: The rise of e-commerce over the past two decades has had a profound impact on consumer spending patterns and the transportation sector. Companies like Amazon have revolutionized the way consumers shop, leading to increased demand for fast and reliable delivery services. As a result, logistics companies like UPS and FedEx, both key components of the DJT, have experienced significant growth in package volumes and revenue. The growth of e-commerce has been a major driver of the DJT's performance, as transportation companies have expanded their operations to meet the rising demand for delivery services. Investors who recognized the potential of e-commerce early on and invested in logistics companies within the DJT have seen substantial gains in their portfolios.

Example: Consumer spending on travel and tourism also plays a significant role in the performance of the DJT, particularly for airlines. During periods of economic growth, consumers are more likely to spend on vacations and leisure activities, leading to increased demand for air travel. For example, in the years following the 2008 financial crisis, as the U.S. economy recovered, consumer spending on travel began to increase, benefiting airlines like Delta Air Lines and Southwest Airlines. The rise in consumer spending on travel contributed to the overall growth of the DJT, as airlines saw higher passenger numbers and increased revenue.

Example: Conversely, during periods of economic uncertainty or decline, consumer spending on travel and discretionary items tends to decrease, negatively impacting the DJT. For instance, during the COVID-19 pandemic, consumer spending on travel and tourism plummeted as people canceled vacations and business trips. Airlines faced a sharp decline in passenger numbers, leading to significant revenue losses and stock price declines. The reduction in consumer spending during the pandemic had a direct impact on the DJT, highlighting the sensitivity of the transportation sector to changes in consumer behavior.

Inflation: The Hidden Cost of Rising Prices

Inflation, or the rate at which the general level of prices for goods and services rises, can have a significant impact on the transportation sector and the DJT. Inflation affects the cost of inputs such as fuel, labor, and raw materials, which can lead to higher operating expenses for transportation companies. Additionally, inflation can erode consumer purchasing power, reducing demand for goods and services and negatively impacting the transportation sector.

Example: The 1970s were marked by a period of high inflation in the United States, driven by factors such as the oil price shocks and increased government spending. This period of "stagflation," where high inflation coincided with stagnant economic growth, had a profound impact on the transportation sector. Airlines, trucking companies, and shipping firms all faced rising fuel costs, which significantly increased their operating expenses. For example, during the 1979 oil crisis, fuel prices surged, leading to higher costs for airlines like American Airlines and trucking companies like J.B. Hunt. The increased costs were difficult to pass on to customers, leading to lower profit margins and declines in stock prices. The high inflation during this period contributed to the overall volatility and underperformance of the DJT.

Example: Inflation can also impact the transportation sector by increasing labor costs. As the cost of living rises, workers demand higher wages to keep up with inflation, leading to increased labor expenses for transportation companies. For instance, during periods of high inflation, unions representing airline pilots, truck drivers, and other transportation workers may negotiate for higher wages and benefits, increasing the operating costs for these companies. The rise in labor costs can squeeze profit margins and lead to lower stock prices for companies within the DJT. Investors who monitor inflation trends and their impact on labor costs within the transportation sector can better manage the risks associated with rising prices.

Example: To mitigate the impact of inflation, some transportation companies within the DJT implement fuel surcharge programs that allow them to pass on a portion of the increased fuel costs to their customers. For example, many trucking companies include fuel surcharges in their freight contracts, which adjust the price of shipping based on changes in fuel prices. Similarly, airlines often add fuel surcharges to ticket prices during periods of rising fuel costs.

These surcharges help transportation companies maintain profitability during periods of high inflation, but they can also lead to higher prices for consumers, potentially reducing demand for transportation services. Investors who understand how companies within the DJT manage inflationary pressures can make more informed investment decisions and better protect their portfolios.

Interest Rates: The Cost of Borrowing

Interest rates, which are set by central banks like the Federal Reserve, have a significant impact on the cost of borrowing for businesses and consumers. Changes in interest rates can influence the transportation sector in several ways, affecting everything from capital expenditures to consumer spending and corporate profitability. The DJT, which includes capital-intensive industries such as airlines, railroads, and shipping companies, is particularly sensitive to changes in interest rates.

Example: During periods of rising interest rates, the cost of borrowing increases for transportation companies, leading to higher expenses for financing new infrastructure, aircraft, and equipment. For example, airlines often rely on debt financing to purchase new planes, expand their fleets, and upgrade their facilities. When interest rates rise, the cost of servicing this debt increases, leading to higher operating expenses and reduced profitability. This can result in lower stock prices for airlines and other transportation companies within the DJT. Investors who monitor interest rate trends and their impact on capital expenditures within the transportation sector can better anticipate potential changes in the DJT's performance.

Example: Interest rates also affect consumer spending, which in turn impacts demand for transportation services. When interest rates rise, consumers face higher borrowing costs for mortgages, auto loans, and credit card debt. This can lead to reduced discretionary spending, including spending on travel and leisure activities. For instance, during periods of high interest rates, consumers may be less likely to take vacations or fly for leisure, leading to lower passenger numbers for airlines. The reduction in consumer spending can negatively impact the DJT, as transportation companies experience reduced demand and lower revenues.

Example: Conversely, during periods of low interest rates, the cost of borrowing decreases, making it easier for transportation companies to finance expansion projects and invest in new technologies. For example, during the period of low interest rates following the 2008 financial crisis, many companies within the DJT took advantage of the favorable borrowing conditions to invest in infrastructure upgrades and fleet expansion. Railroads like Union Pacific and Norfolk Southern invested in new locomotives, tracks, and technology to improve efficiency and capacity. Airlines also expanded their fleets and upgraded their facilities to meet growing demand. The lower interest rates supported increased capital expenditures and contributed to the overall growth of the DJT during the economic recovery.

Exchange Rates: The Impact of Currency Fluctuations

Exchange rates, which determine the value of one currency relative to another, play a crucial role in the transportation sector, particularly for companies engaged in international trade. Fluctuations in exchange rates can impact the cost of goods, the competitiveness of exports, and the profitability of companies within the DJT.

Example: A strong U.S. dollar can have mixed effects on the transportation sector. On the one hand, a strong dollar makes imports cheaper, which can increase demand for shipping services as more goods are brought into the country. For example, shipping companies like FedEx and UPS, which handle a significant volume of international freight, may benefit from increased import activity when the dollar is strong. On the other hand, a strong dollar can make U.S. exports more expensive for foreign buyers, potentially reducing demand for goods transported by railroads and shipping companies. For instance, if the dollar strengthens against the euro, U.S. agricultural exports to Europe may become less competitive, leading to lower demand for rail transport and a negative impact on the DJT.

Example: Conversely, a weak U.S. dollar can boost U.S. exports by making American goods more affordable for foreign buyers. This can increase demand for transportation services, particularly for companies involved in exporting goods overseas. For example, during periods of a weak dollar, companies like Kansas City Southern, which operates a rail network connecting the U.S. with Mexico, may see increased demand for cross-border freight services as U.S. exports to Mexico rise. Similarly, shipping companies may benefit from higher export volumes, contributing to the overall performance of the DJT. Investors who monitor exchange rate trends and their impact on international trade can gain valuable insights into the potential performance of the DJT.

Example: Exchange rate fluctuations can also impact the cost structure of transportation companies with international operations. For instance, airlines that purchase fuel and aircraft in foreign currencies may face higher costs if the value of the dollar declines. Similarly, shipping companies that operate in multiple regions may face currency risk when converting earnings from foreign operations back into U.S. dollars. To manage this risk, some transportation companies use hedging strategies, such as forward contracts or currency swaps, to lock in exchange rates and protect against adverse currency movements. Investors who understand how companies within the DJT manage currency risk can better assess the potential impact of exchange rate fluctuations on their investments.

Conclusion: Mastering the Nasdaq DJT and Embracing the Future

The Nasdaq DJT (Dow Jones Transportation Average) serves as a powerful barometer for the transportation sector, reflecting the economic forces, market dynamics, and industry-specific trends that drive this crucial segment of the global economy. Throughout this book, we have explored the intricate relationships between the DJT and various macroeconomic indicators, the impact of economic cycles, investment strategies, risk management techniques, and the influence of technological advancements. By understanding these factors, investors can better navigate the complexities of the transportation sector and make informed decisions that align with their financial goals.

The transportation sector is a cornerstone of economic activity, and its performance provides valuable insights into the health and direction of the broader economy. The DJT, with its diverse components ranging from airlines and railroads to trucking and logistics companies, offers a unique lens through which to view the interconnections between different industries and economic indicators. By analyzing the DJT, investors can gain a deeper understanding of how the transportation sector responds to changes in GDP growth, consumer spending, inflation, interest rates, and other key economic variables.

Moreover, the strategies outlined in this book—whether focused on broad exposure through ETFs, sector rotation, individual stock selection, or risk management—provide a comprehensive toolkit for navigating the DJT. By applying these strategies, investors can capitalize on opportunities within the transportation sector while mitigating potential risks. The examples provided throughout the chapters illustrate how these strategies can be effectively implemented, offering practical insights into real-world investment scenarios.

The Future of the DJT: The Role of Artificial Intelligence

As we look to the future, one of the most significant forces that will shape the transportation sector and, by extension, the Nasdaq DJT, is the rapid advancement of artificial intelligence (AI). AI has the potential to revolutionize the transportation industry in ways that were previously unimaginable, impacting everything from operational efficiency and logistics to customer experience and market dynamics.

AI and Operational Efficiency: AI is already being integrated into various aspects of the transportation sector to improve operational efficiency. For example, AI-powered predictive maintenance systems are being used by railroads and airlines to monitor the condition of equipment in real time, identifying potential issues before they lead to costly breakdowns or delays. By reducing downtime and optimizing maintenance schedules, these AI systems can significantly enhance the efficiency and reliability of transportation networks, ultimately benefiting companies within the DJT.

AI and Autonomous Vehicles: The development of autonomous vehicles, driven by advances in AI, has the potential to transform the trucking and logistics industries. Companies like Tesla and Waymo are leading the charge in creating self-driving trucks and delivery vehicles that promise to reduce labor costs, increase safety, and improve delivery times. As these technologies become more widespread, they could lead to significant shifts in the transportation sector, with companies that successfully adopt and integrate AI-powered autonomous vehicles gaining a competitive edge. This, in turn, could have a profound impact on the composition and performance of the DJT, as the transportation landscape evolves.

AI and Supply Chain Optimization: AI is also playing a crucial role in optimizing supply chains by analyzing vast amounts of data to predict demand, manage inventory, and streamline logistics. AI algorithms can identify the most efficient routes for shipping, anticipate disruptions due to weather or geopolitical events, and adjust supply chain strategies in real time. This level of optimization can lead to cost savings and improved service levels for companies within the DJT, enhancing their profitability and market performance. As AI continues to advance, its impact on supply chain management is likely to become even more pronounced, driving further innovation in the transportation sector.

AI and Market Analysis: For investors, AI is becoming an increasingly valuable tool for analyzing market trends and making investment decisions. AI-driven algorithms can process vast amounts of financial data, identify patterns, and generate insights that would be difficult for human analysts to discern. By applying AI to the analysis of the DJT, investors can gain a more comprehensive understanding of market dynamics, anticipate shifts in the transportation sector, and make more informed investment decisions. AI can also be used to develop more sophisticated risk management strategies, helping investors navigate the complexities of the DJT with greater confidence.

Embracing the Future

As the transportation sector continues to evolve, the Nasdaq DJT will remain a critical indicator of economic health and industry performance. By staying attuned to the macroeconomic indicators, market dynamics, and technological advancements that influence the DJT, investors can position themselves to take advantage of the opportunities within this vital sector.

The future of the DJT is one of innovation and transformation, driven by forces such as AI, globalization, and changing consumer preferences. As AI continues to reshape the transportation industry, its impact on the DJT will become increasingly significant. Investors who embrace these changes and leverage AI-driven insights will be well-positioned to navigate the complexities of the transportation sector and achieve their financial objectives.

In conclusion, mastering the Nasdaq DJT requires a deep understanding of the economic forces, investment strategies, and technological trends that shape the transportation sector. By applying the knowledge and strategies outlined in this book, investors can confidently navigate the DJT, manage risks, and capitalize on the opportunities that lie ahead. As we move into an era of rapid technological advancement, the ability to adapt and embrace new innovations, such as AI, will be key to staying ahead in the ever-evolving landscape of the transportation sector.

www.ingramcontent.com/pod-product-compliance
Lightning Source LLC
Chambersburg PA
CBHW062112220526
45471CB00010B/3699